SEXUAL STRANGERS

In the series

Queer Politics, Queer Theories

edited by Shane Phelan

SEXUAL STRANGERS

GAYS, LESBIANS,

AND DILEMMAS

OF CITIZENSHIP

Shane Phelan

 Temple University Press
PHILADELPHIA

Temple University Press, Philadelphia 19122
Copyright © 2001 by Temple University
All rights reserved
Published 2001
Printed in the United States of America

Library of Congress Cataloging-in-Publication Data

Phelan, Shane.
  Sexual strangers : gays, lesbians, and dilemmas of citizenship / Shane Phelan.
    p. cm. — (Queer politics, queer theories)
  Includes bibliographical references and index.
  ISBN 1-56639-827-4 (cloth : alk. paper) — ISBN 1-56639-828-2 (pbk. : alk. paper)
    1. Gay rights—United States. 2. Political rights—United States. 3. Citizenship—United States. 4. Homosexuality—Political aspects—United States. 5. Lesbianism—Political aspects—United States. I. Title. II. Series.

HQ76.8.U5 P48 2001
305.9'0664'0973—dc21   00-032564

To Den, finally—
another stranger, another home

Contents

Acknowledgments

As is always the case, many other people worked to make this book better than it would have been. Jodi Dean, Kathleen Jones, Morris Kaplan, and David Rayside each read an earlier version of the manuscript and made suggestions and comments far beyond the call of duty. Annalise Acorn, Nico Beger, Christine Di Stefano, Kathy Ferguson, Judith Garber, Jonathan Goldberg-Hiller, Victoria Gray, Cheryl Hall, Susan Hekman, and Rogers Smith read chapters and offered their insights. If I have not always followed their advice, it is a sign not of ingratitude but of stubbornness. Audiences at the universities of California–Los Angeles, Colorado, Hawai'i, Nevada–Las Vegas, New Mexico, and Wichita State, and at numerous conferences helped me clarify my thinking. Several anonymous reviewers helped, especially where I least liked what they had to say. Doris Braendel at Temple University Press has been editor, co-conspirator, and friend.

I have been fortunate to have two fine graduate students through the years of this writing. Judy Palier's enthusiasm and willingness to try on new ideas has continually spurred me to think about what I am saying. Don Westervelt has offered that rare opportunity for many academics, a student from whom I have learned and whose work spurs my own. As I finish this book, and they finish their dissertations, I am grateful to have shared this process with them.

A slightly revised version of Chapter 2 appeared as "Bodies, Passions, and Citizenship," *Critical Review of International Social and Political Philosophy* 2/1 (1999): 56-79. Material from Chapter 3 will appear as "Queering Democracy: Citizenship and Kinship" in Sabine Hark, ed., *Queering Democracy* (Hamburg: Querverlag, 2000). Parts of Chapter 4 appeared in "Public Discourse and the Closeting of Butch Lesbians," in *Butch/ Femme: Theorizing Lesbian Gender*, ed. Sally Munt (Herndon, Va.: Cassell Academic, 1998), and in "The Shape of Queer: Articulation and Assimilation," *Women and Politics* 18/2 (1997): 55-73. I am grateful to the publishers for permission to reprint.

SEXUAL STRANGERS

Introduction

s the United States a heterosexual regime? If it is, how might
we understand the political position of those who cannot or
will not align themselves with heterosexuality? Are such persons citizens, albeit stigmatized and embattled ones, or are
they more fundamentally excluded from membership in the
U.S. polity? What social and political institutions structure
the regime of heterosexuality? Can sexual minorities refigure those institutions enough to make room for themselves
in them, or will they find themselves continually stuck
between the pressure to conform and rejection of their best
efforts?

We live in a time of new challenges and opportunities.
We are faced with global warming and environmental degradation, increasing dominance by international corporations
and global media, and the weakening of the nation-state
even as more peoples aspire to achieve statehood. In the
United States, the last thirty years have witnessed massive
shifts in politics and culture: Watergate; the end of the Viet-
nam conflict, inaugurating endless mourning; the New
World Order in which, in place of the Soviet Union, we have
everything and everyone to fear; the rise of the New Right;
and, contrapuntally, of feminism, as well as racial and ethnic
political movements and environmental movements.

Not the least important of these developments is the
growth of lesbian and gay visibility. In 1968, homosexuals
were barely a blip on America's radar screen. Aside from

1

their occasional utility in political campaigns and vendettas, in which one contestant accused the other of being "soft on perverts," homosexuals were either ignored or laughed at. Since 1969, gays and lesbians have come to figure centrally in American debates about national identity, equality, and values. From news coverage that is increasingly balanced to the ubiquitous visibility of gays, lesbians, bisexuals, and transgendered people on tabloid talk shows, America gets a steady and varied diet of homosexuality (Alwood 1996; Bennett 1998; Cook 1999; Gamson 1998). AIDS put gay men in the spotlight, in a number of roles: promiscuous death-dealers, benighted individual sufferers, responsible activists, devoted lovers and friends. The activism generated by groups such as ACT-UP offered sharp contrasts to stereotypes of passive partygoers. Fights for access to the military and for the right to marry put lesbians and gays in the position of oppressed minorities seeking equal access to core institutions, solid citizens who want only to be included. The growth of mass markets for gay and lesbian studies and popular literature signals an increased ability and willingness to be "out."

This new visibility has not, of course, been uncontested. The end of the Soviet Union and their need for a specter to fight led the New Right to focus on gays as a national threat (Herman 1997). Drives for legal protection have led to backlash movements to ban non-discrimination laws, most famously in Colorado's Amendment 2 of 1992 but also in Oregon, Idaho, and cities across the United States. The Supreme Court's ruling that Amendment 2 was unconstitutional did not eliminate these drives, and later rulings have made clear that laws barring non-discrimination are acceptable to the Court.

The fights over marriage and the military have increasingly defined "the lesbian and gay rights movement." Another long-term battle, for a national bill to ban discrimination in housing and employment, has been conducted largely in the shadows of these two titanic struggles. On its face this is a curious situation. While most Americans now express support for employment non-discrimination, ambivalence rises for military inclusion and peaks into resistance to "gay marriage." (Nor is this dynamic exclusive to heterosexuals. Gays, lesbians, and bisexuals have always had vigorous debates about whether marriage and the military were things to which we should aspire. Increasingly, however, mainstream movement leaders are calling for an end to such debates.

Whether or not one wants to enlist in either institution, they argue, we must fight for everyone's right to participate if they so choose. This liberal argument has proven very hard to resist in this liberal land, though some [e.g., Warner 1999] continue to do so.) An observer might then expect that the Employment Non-Discrimination Act would not only be at the top of the agenda for organizations, but would also be relatively easy to achieve. The obscurity and difficulty facing such a bill is explicable when we account for several factors. The first is the composition and funding base of the national gay and lesbian political organizations. By and large the constituency of groups such as the Human Rights Campaign, while often forced into "the closet" at work, live their work lives relatively unobstructed by their sexual orientation. Those most typically affected by homophobia at work—butch lesbians and fem men—are, as we will see, not only under-served by such organizations, they are implicitly disavowed. The issues of marriage and military service, on the other hand, do directly affect supporters of the national organizations. This is not the only reason for the centrality of these issues to 1990s organization and debate, but it is one major factor.

The second reason for the importance of these issues is their perceived link to citizenship. Indeed, citizenship is the central concept appealed to in calls for inclusion. This is not surprising. U.S. citizenship has always embodied dreams of living one's life as one chooses while also being gainfully employed and willing to serve if called (Shklar 1991; Smith 1997). More broadly, citizenship is about recognition and participation. Citizenship is not unique in this; all groups necessarily highlight recognition and participation as desirable goals. As membership in the modern nation-state, however, citizenship is unique for what recognition entails. Citizenship is supposed to guarantee both fair treatment at home and protection abroad. It implies that one's government, and one's fellow citizens, concern themselves with one's welfare and one's opinions. Such concern does not mandate a particular policy on farm or housing subsidies, for example, but it does require that the individual(s) in question not be denied the recognition embodied in central institutions and universal services such as police protection.

The press of contemporary events as well as recent developments in political theory have brought citizenship to the center of attention. A category that once languished has had a rebirth of astonishing vitality.

There are several reasons for this renaissance. The growth of communitarian challenges to liberalism (Barber 1984; Etzioni 1995; Sandel 1982; Taylor 1985) and the huge growth of interest in the work of Hannah Arendt (Benhabib 1992; Disch 1994; Hinchman and Hinchman 1994; Honig 1995), as well as feminist political theory's challenge to public/private divides, have mandated fresh examination of the public sphere (Phillips 1991; Mouffe 1993; Honig 1995). In the United States and throughout Europe, citizenship has become a pressing issue as immigrants are attacked and citizens of non-European heritage are denied equality in the name of ethnic nationalities. Simultaneously, gays and lesbians are demanding that the nation-states in which they hold legal citizenship offer them the same rights of citizenship offered to others.

As these fights intensify, it has become clear that the concept of citizenship has lost none of its power, but that its place in our common life is not a settled one. Citizenship is a powerful political ideal as well as a legal status. The debates in political theory have in many ways been irrelevant to these current struggles, because theorists have weighed the merits of republican versus liberal citizenship as modes of participation and identification while debates in policy and law have focused on legal status. All of these venues have important insights to offer about citizenship, and it behooves us to consider them together rather than in isolation.

Citizenship studies have also produced a new consideration of exclusion. Most political theory addresses itself only to those presumed to be "within" a given polity, considering how and whether citizens are equal, what citizens owe one another, what the state owes its citizens, and so on. Recent work has begun to acknowledge that modern states contain huge numbers of people who are not citizens, and that these people must be considered in some way other than as a "problem" for citizens. Conceptualizing these non-citizens is not always easy. Often they are treated as citizens of another state, as if reading their passports answers the question of belonging. But many today are "passport citizens" of countries that do not account for them in their public life except as those "others" who trouble the body politic. In his work on European Jews, Zygmunt Bauman (1991) has developed the concept of the "stranger," neither us nor clearly them, not friend and not enemy, but a figure of ambivalence who troubles the border between us and them. The enemy is the clear opposite of the citizen, but the stranger is more fraught with anxiety.

I will argue through this book that lesbians, gays, bisexuals, and transgendered people in the United States are strangers. The category of the stranger enables us to better understand both the current citizenship status of lesbian, gay, and bisexual persons in the United States and the strategies of entry of the recent past. I will argue that lesbians and gay men are not currently citizens in the full political sense, and that this exclusion is at the core of contemporary American understandings and organization of common life. Understanding the extent to which heterosexuality is a prerequisite for modern citizenship illuminates the lives of all who value and aspire to citizenship.

Sexual minorities are not citizens of the United States even in the thin terms of liberal theory. As a category that is both legal and political, and whose political dimensions are multifaceted, citizenship is a matter of several elements. Laws guaranteeing equal protection and the right of participation are a sine qua non for citizenship, both because they enact or deny state acknowledgment of individuals and because such rights are a prerequisite for meaningful participation. The state's reluctance to protect lesbians and gay men from violence, although decreasing, continues to be quite stunning both at the level of individual police and, more tellingly, among politicians, many of whom are reluctant to endorse hate crimes legislation if sexual orientation is included. If individuals cannot rely upon the protection of the laws, they cannot fully participate in public affairs. Such laws signal the willingness of the state (and, in a democracy, the people) to accord equal respect even to those with whom they differ on crucial issues. Citizenship does not require the active approval and communion of others, but it does require an affirmation of one's place in the political community.

After delineating an idea of citizenship rooted not in formal equality but in acknowledgment, I argue that sexual minorities are better understood as strangers, not enemies but not friends or "natives" either. The stranger's strangeness may be formally denied in liberal regimes, but her distance from cultural membership makes her continually prey to renewed exclusion, scapegoating, and violence.

The contests over marriage and the military offer us a window into citizenship and the construction of national strangers. Usually parties to the debate have presumed the importance of marriage and military service to citizenship and have argued about whether lesbians and gays should want to participate. Less often, however, have lesbian and gay writers turned to look the other way, to question critically the relation between these institutions and citizenship. That does not mean that no one has, however. Feminists have struggled over the last thirty years to clarify the linkages between the "public" institutions of citizenship and military service and the "private" ones of family and work. In order to see what citizenship implies and presupposes, and how sexual strangers are produced in political discourse, I turn in Chapter 2 to feminist discussions of citizenship, bodies, and passions. Chapter 3 continues this path by considering what anthropological work on kinship can tell us about the citizenship stakes of the marriage question. What is the package that some so desperately wish to keep from lesbians and gays, and that others want so much? Unwrapping it will help us understand both desires.

As important as these institutions are, they are not the sum of citizenship. Citizenship is about participation in the social and political life of a political community, and as such it is not confined to a list of legal protections and inclusions. It is just as much about political and cultural visibility. "Visibility," of course, is not one thing, nor is it necessarily and always good. Assertions that visibility is essential to gay and lesbian citizenship, like arguments about the visibility of blacks and other minorities, introduce further questions: Who among these diverse groups is to be visible? Is all visibility good? Certainly, many gay activists are profoundly uneasy with the images they see on TV and in print media following any pride march, or any week on a talk show. Visibility as a goal is also potentially bound to consumption and advanced capitalism at least as much as to political membership (Hennessy 1995). Strategies such as kiss-ins, celebrated by some as radical infusions of queer desire into public space, serve to reinforce perceived distance between homosexuality and citizenship as they subvert notions of "appropriate" displays of sexuality. Public spaces are occupied not only by citizens, but also by enemies and strangers to the nation-state. Visibility is no guarantee of either citizenship or equality. Visibility is, however, essential on one level. A group that is consistently present only as the opposite or the outside of the nation, that has no part in the national imaginary except as threat, cannot participate in citizenship, no matter what rights its members have come to enjoy. It is at this level of the national imaginary that gays, lesbians, and bisexuals are most thoroughly sexual strangers. By "the national imaginary" I do not mean to posit one way of thinking in which all members of a nation participate, but rather the persistent cluster of images and rhetoric that, however inadequately and imperfectly, signal to a population who and what it is. There are, in this sense, always overlapping and contradictory national imaginaries; yet some are hegemonic over others, carrying with them the weight of cultural, economic, and political dominance of certain groups. Thus, although most Hispanics in the United States see themselves as fully American, dominant discourses and imaginaries figure them as threats who must be contained via border patrols, immigration quotas, cutbacks on social services, and English-only schools. This threat is balanced, however, by the increasing visibility of Hispanics in government, culture, and business, forcing the image of the United States as "land of opportunity" to confront that of the United States as "white man's empire."

Many liberals (in both the classical and contemporary uses of that word) see the growth of visibility and participation by racial minorities and women as evidence of the inevitable progress of reason and tolerance in liberal regimes. They might justifiably expect the same for sexual minorities—indeed, many do. The heightened visibility of gays and lesbians in the United States suggests that a time will come when the image of the United States as God's Christian nation will have to confront an image of inclusion. This does not, for many, mean that the United States will become less Christian, but that its Christianity will become kinder and gentler, focusing on Jesus's message of love rather than Paul's fear and vitriol. For others, the desired future will find religion to be a wholly private matter, governing individual actions but not policy. In that nation, diverse readings of the Bible, Torah, or Koran might shape views on sexuality, but those views will not spill over into one's treatment of others in the market, workplace, or government.

I am not optimistic that such a solution is either desirable or possible. Chapter 4 examines recent forays into public discourse and media visibility and argues that they have largely operated by essentializing sexual orientation, privatizing sex, and downplaying gender deviance. Thus, the growth of "respectable" public media, although an important advance, has simultaneously created secondary sets of strangers among lesbians and gays. This is in accord with Cathy Cohen's thesis (1999) that "advanced marginalization," in which groups begin to gain some access for elite members, intensifies "secondary marginalization" within stigmatized communities. Chapter 5 discusses this process in reference to the new stigmatization of bisexuals and transgendered people. This new stigmatization has several faces. One face openly scapegoats bi and trans people to claim the relative normality of lesbians and gays (Gamson 1998). The other appears to be inclusive, but continually subsumes bi and trans experiences and perspectives within the model of homosexuality. Neither strategy confronts the ways in which sexual strangeness continue to be generated, and so, I argue, they will not work in the end for even the most "normal" gay or lesbian people.

Instead of a flight from strangeness, a broad commitment to "queering" citizenship is in order. Rather than flee from strangeness, sexual strangers may offer one another and others new ways of questioning the current tight fabric of citizenship and national identity. Chapter 6 returns to the question of citizenship to examine recent suggestions for more democratic and inclusive regimes. These suggestions continue to be limited, in ways that are perhaps inevitable to institutional politics, by either failing to consider difference seriously enough or by treating it as neatly bounded and fixed. I argue that before political/legal citizenship can be achieved a thorough queering of public culture is needed. My suggestions for the nature of that queering are just a beginning, an outline that others are shaping and filling in practice. I hope instead to convince students of politics, both academic and activist, that strategies of equality (crucial as they are) must always be attuned to the difference between equality and sameness. The position of the stranger is not only difficult, it is rewarding. Let us not abandon it for a citizenship that abandons others and suffocates that in each of us that does not fit; instead, I hope to help imagine and enact a postmodern citizenship of solidarity from the inside(r) out, in which many bodies, many passions, many families, many workers, find a place.

As the attentive reader will find, my main inspiration for critical analysis is feminist theory. One way of describing the shortcomings of contemporary movement politics is to say that the success of an autonomous "gay and lesbian" movement has come at the price of the loss of more thoroughgoing feminist commitments on the part of lesbians (and many gay men) in favor of a "me-too" liberal feminism that has always made the same mistakes described in this book. Feminist theorists are the ones who have most thoroughly pursued questions of the body (female, male, and other); of the role of passion in public life; of inequality within and through family structures; and of citizenship. Certainly some of these theorists and scholars are lesbian or queer, and certainly many heterosexual feminists have overlooked lesbian configurations of body, gender, and desire. Nonetheless, it is their continuing attention to women and gender that has provided so much insight. Certainly there is a growing body of work by men on masculinity and gender that is proving important, but much of that work is explicitly feminist or indebted to feminist scholarship as well. This does not mean that in the end there is nothing to queer theory or lesbian and gay studies that isn't done better by feminist studies; it means that queer work that does not pay attention to feminist theory, that abandons feminist work as the boring essentialist mother of the postmodern queer, is fated to fall prey to the traps of liberal/republican citizenship outlined in this book.

For reasons that will become clearer throughout the book, I believe that sexual minorities will remain strangers in the United States for a long time to come. This is so not because the United States is a particularly Puritan country (although it is, in many ways), but because of the particular configuration of citizenship that we have conjured here. Moving toward citizenship for sexual minorities will require not just an expansion of some boundaries, but a wholesale rethinking of the relations among citizenship, family, masculinity, religion, and sexuality. Nor am I sanguine that such rethinking is on the horizon. This is not, I realize, a conclusion that will please most readers. It flies in the face of other quintessentially American values such as optimism, and it will sound to some like embracing victimhood. It is nonetheless the only honest answer I have at this point. The history of other strangers, most notably the painful dance of assimilation and annihilation of Jews in Europe, demonstrates that strangers cannot assume that history moves only in one direction. The re-ignition of hostilities between Serbs and virtually everyone they define as a stranger, new waves of killings of Jewish children in Los Angeles, neo-Nazi renaissance in the United States and Europe, and the rise of anti-gay violence make clear that no gains are final or unequivocal.

Does this mean there is no hope? Hardly. But hope is not born of rational calculation of probable outcomes; it is a renewable resource that springs in defiance of such outcomes to move individuals to act as though success were likely. I am not, then, advising quiescence or the abandonment of political activism of all stripes. My aim here is to encourage readers to take seriously the task of becoming citizens, which means confronting the full weight of the barriers to that state. Strategies that bypass cultural institutions in favor of a thin liberal citizenship will inevitably prove as weak as thin liberalism has in motivating citizens to extend their privileges to those currently lacking them. We can—we must—do better.

Citizens and Strangers

itizenship has a long history, both as a legal concept and as a political ideal. It is "a weighty, monumental, humanist word," speaking "of respect, of rights, of dignity" (Fraser and Gordon 1998, 113). Yet, as Peter Riesenberg (1992, xvi) has observed, "there is no single office in which its essence is defined. It has no central mission, nor is it clearly an office, a theory, or a legal contract." Despite its status as an "ambiguous institution" (xvii), however, citizenship is a primary, perhaps *the* primary, modern category of political membership.

The association of citizenship with democracy and self-governance is a modern phenomenon. From the Roman Empire to modern times, citizenship was not clearly distinct from subjecthood. Through the liberal and republican traditions, citizenship came to mean both the legal status of state membership and a specific claim to participate in public affairs as an equal; as J.G.A. Pocock (1998, 34) puts it, participants in modern liberal democracies "believe that the individual denied decision in shaping her or his life is being denied treatment as a human, and that citizenship—meaning membership in some public and political frame of action—is necessary if we are to be granted decision and empowered to be human."

Interwoven with the empowerment of citizenship, however, has been the exclusion of those seen as outside the polity or unfit for membership: "it is no exaggeration to say that one of its principal functions has been as an agent or principle of discrimination" (Riesenberg 1992, xvii). The stronger the pre-sumed bond between citizens, the greater the need for exclusion to main-tain cohesion and ways of life. This dynamic of membership and exclusion has continually presented challenges for those who would become citizens, as they are forced to explain why their membership claims are more worthy than those of others. In the United States, per-haps most famously and disastrously for later feminism, white female suf-fragists sought southern support by appealing to the threat of black males and other racial "invaders" and "polluters" whose votes needed to be bal-anced by the power of white womanhood (Davis 1983; hooks 1981). Post-colonial debates about citizenship have focused on attempts by former metropoles to define their members (Brubaker 1998; Smith 1994b) as well as the construction of a new European citizenship (Dubiel 1998; Habermas 1995; Lehning 1998; Preuss 1998; Tassin 1992). These debates remind us that the empowerment of citizenship is always bought with expulsion.

Feminist theorists have also considered the nature of citizenship throughout the past ten years (Alexander 1991, 1994; Curthoys 1993; Jones 1997, 1998; Lister 1997; Mouffe 1993; Vogel 1991, 1994). This work has moved from rejecting citizenship as an exclusive, hierarchical ideal to attempts to negotiate its dilemmas. The very real protections afforded by citizenship have become salient as women strive for voice and recognition within nation-states. Nonetheless, feminist work has been sharply critical of citizenship both as an ideal and as a practice.

I begin from these debates in order to discuss both the importance of citizenship and the conflicts encountered by groups trying to become citizens in polities that do not want them. In order to understand the ways in which sexual minorities are not yet citizens, or not fully such, in the United States, we must step back to consider the nature of citi-zenship itself. Doing so will enable us to see the ways in which official citizens may nonetheless be civic strangers.

Citizenship as Acknowledgment

Citizenship embodies several elements, none dispensable, but each differently highlighted by different traditions. While the liberal tradi-tion has focused on legal protection of civil rights, the republican tradition of citizenship, dating at least from Aristotle, locates citizenship in the activity of ruling and being ruled in turn (or, in Rousseau's ideal, simultaneously). Here the citizen is not simply the subject of a sovereign and its laws, nor just a consumer of rights and privileges, but is an active member in the public deliberation and decision-making that produces law and policy. In this understanding the citizen is not simply one whose passport says "Italy" or "Great Britain," but one with the right (indeed, the obligation) to participate in civic affairs. In the republican tradition, "citizenship is an activity or a practice, and not simply a status, so that not to engage in the practice is, in important senses, not to be a citizen" (Oldfield 1998, 79). Of course, one's ability and willingness to engage in the practice(s) of citizenship will be shaped by others' reception and acknowledgment of one's presence and participation. The republican tradition, with its admirable focus on activity and participation, has also historically offered grounds for the exclusion of many that liberal/legal thinkers might allow. From Aristotle's denial of citizenship to workers to land, property, literacy, race, and gender requirements for participation, the republican tradition has provided robust visions of participation inextricably bound to robust exclusions of those seen as unfit.

Even as we agree with republicans on the importance of practice for citizenship, we can question "what qualifies as the behavior of citizens" (Jones 1998, 223). Long conceived in terms of masculine prerogatives such as voting, holding office, and speaking in public, citizenship has been re-envisioned by feminist theorists as encompassing many of the activities of care and world-maintaining that had been relegated to "the private" (Jones 1997, 1998; Lister 1997; Mouffe 1993; Sarvasy 1997; Sparks 1997; Tronto 1993). Recent queer theory has also extended citizenship to stress public discourse about sexuality (Berlant 1997). Thus the category of citizenship seems to open up under the pressure of multiple desires to identify with its promises.

Whether we view citizenship as legal status or as practice, we might understand it as affording individuals a certain protection for their interests. The particular articulation of which interests count as public varies across place and time, but the capacity to articulate one's interests as a matter for public concern is a defining mark of citizenship. Citizenship is more than this protection, however; as Jean Leca (1992, 20) explains, it "establishes a double relation in terms of interests. On the one hand, it is derived from interests. . . . But, on the other hand, citizenship is also a resource which permits more of the socially disempowered to acquire a greater political competence." From the perspective of this "double relation," citizenship is a crucial sign under which members mobilize for common interest and, in so doing, acquire more than private gains. As citizens, individuals make a particular kind of claim on other citizens even as they commit themselves to recognizing others as citizens. As V. Spike Peterson and Laura Parisi (1997, 8) put it, "in contemporary states the well-being of individuals is linked to citizenship claims that mark who is inside (and outside) of the state's responsibility for protecting rights and providing welfare." Citizenship status is the basic indicator of membership; the specific rights and obligations of citizens may vary from state to state, but recognition as members is prerequisite to a claim on any configuration of rights and duties.

The distinction between legal status and political membership is thus not the same as that between civil and political rights. Political membership is a matter of both civil and political rights, but it extends beyond those rights to inclusion in public culture. To capture the dilemma of stigmatized and marginalized persons within a society with few legal barriers to equality, we must examine rights, offices, and duties as aspects of a larger phenomenon of political membership. The question of citizenship does not concern only what rights, offices, and duties are to accrue to citizens, but also how the polity decides who is eligible for them; that is, it concerns the structures of acknowledgment that define the class of persons eligible for those rights, offices, and duties.

Webster's Third New International Dictionary defines the verb "acknowledge" as follows: "to show by word or act that one has knowledge of and respect for the rights, claims, authority or status of"; "recognize, honor, or respect, esp. publicly"; "making known to others or recognizing to one's self what might be kept back, suppressed, or left uncertain, esp. under the influence of stress, pressure, or persuasion." These definitions lead us to an understanding of the role of acknowledgment in citizenship. Acknowledgment is not a right in itself, but the establishment of a particular political relation. The enactment of citizenship is itself the recognition that one has a claim to be heard and responded to—that one should be acknowledged. Citizenship is embodied in one's access to rights and other institutions, but it is not identical to those rights and institutions. It is the emergence into publicity as an equal with other citizens. What exactly is being acknowledged in citizenship, and how does this pertain to the position of sexual minorities? The first definition, demonstrating by word or deed the "knowledge of and respect for the rights, claims, authority or status of," seems tailor-made for citizenship. Insofar as we understand citizenship as a matter of rights, claims, authority, and status, acknowledgment as a citizen would seem to be a matter of acceptance and endorsement of these for the group in question. Such acceptance and endorsement need not extend to personal embrace, but it must include active willingness to defend those rights, claims, authority, and status; it must include willingness to "recognize, honor, respect" in public.

Current controversy over the position of lesbians, gays, and bisexuals in the United States makes clear, as perhaps few other controversies can, the relation between the first definition, what might be called "political acknowledgment" as many would understand it, and the definitions that follow. The idea of "coming out," and the closet to which it is contrasted, has become such a paradigm for "making known to others or recognizing to oneself what might be kept back, suppressed, or left uncertain" that people now use the phrase "come out" to describe virtually any revelation about themselves. In contrast with most women and racial minorities, sexual minorities have a varying ability to be hidden, to leave their difference "suppressed or left uncertain." And this is how many, if not most, heterosexuals would like them to remain. Many who express support for the legal rights of sexual minorities nonetheless voice the desire that "those people" keep their difference invisible (Gamson 1998, ch. 6). This demonstrates either a disjuncture between the first meaning of acknowledgment and the latter ones, or— as I will argue—the fragility and unworkability of the first without the latter. The classical liberal solution of support for rights without social acceptance fails to capture the dilemma of citizenship for all cultural minorities.

What exactly is being acknowledged in the acknowledgment of citizenship? Full citizenship requires that one be recognized not in spite of one's unusual or minority characteristics, but with those characteristics understood as part of a valid possibility for the conduct of life. Emergence into publicity as an equal means that one appears on the terms by which one understands oneself—that one be an active co-constructor of one's public appearance. In Dan Diner's (1998, 300) words, the core of citizenship is "the values and grounds of communal loyalty and solidarity." In addition to the legal acknowledgment by the state that is part of subjecthood, citizenship involves the "will and the capacity to participate in a common undertaking, i.e., to cooperate and to communicate with the other members, to recognize them as equals, and to be recognized by them as an equal" (Preuss 1998, 313). I may be discussed in public, brought into a certain visibility, without being acknowledged. Of course, emergence into publicity does not mean that I will be the sole constructor, or have final say over the constructions made of my appearance; citizenship cannot require simple endorsement of every identity that may emerge, and, as we will see, regimes define themselves partly by the range of identities and understandings that they will accept. But mere visibility is also not enough. Later chapters will address the variety of ways that lesbians and gays tried to emerge in American publicity in the 1990s and will find that many of them fail to recognize the dynamics of co-construction. For now, it must be enough to say that who is acknowledged and who is not in a particular regime is not only an issue for the groups who are left out, but provides clues into the constitutive assumptions of the regime, often unknown to or unacknowledged by its members.

An example of the role of acknowledgment in citizenship is the host of current elementary school programs operating under the name "Character Counts." Such programs aim to instill certain social virtues through discussion and action. Among the seven virtues singled out for attention, along with responsibility, discipline, and others, is citizenship. In Character Counts, citizenship is not a status conferred by the law but rather a quality of the person that is manifested in certain actions. These actions extend beyond those available only to adults, such as voting, that have been held out as the quintessence of citizenship. Rather, they include a general concern and respect for others as well as participation in public affairs. Such respect is inseparable from acknowledgment of others as valuable, distinct members of a community. In turn, participation in the community presupposes the acknowledgment by others of one's membership; without such acknowledgment one may force others to notice oneself, but one cannot claim membership. One may be noticed as an enemy, or an outsider; being a citizen requires not only notice but acknowledgment.

The Character Counts definition also suggests that citizenship is not something that is simply conferred on an individual, but is something that must be developed. It also points to the ways in which one person's citizenship is bound to another's. If one person fails to manifest concern and respect for others, that is by this definition a failure of her citizenship, not a reflection on others. Yet the centrality of acknowledgment to citizenship suggests that the failure of one person to act as a citizen makes the citizenship of others more precarious. This is indeed the case, as is recognized in much democratic theory. It is of particular relevance here because it points to the dependence of sexual minorities on the citizenship of majorities. If declining mutual concern and respect are an issue for the American polity in general, that will lessen the chances for minorities in particular to receive the acknowledgment that citizens require.

The laws and customs of countries flesh out the meaning of citizenship in a particular polity. To be deprived of the protection of those laws, or to be barred from meaningful participation in the institutions and practices of that country, is to be denied the acknowledgment that is the heart of citizenship. Sometimes individuals may be denied such protection and participation on the basis of ascriptive characteristics, such as when women are denied equal rights to those of men; at other times, denial occurs through (non)enforcement of the laws, as when African-Americans were denied voting rights through selective literacy testing. In such instances, rights claims are an effective way to articulate the failure of the polity and to demand inclusion. Still, the question of citizenship is not simply a rights question, but is rather one of a claim on the public attention and concern. Rights are not simply legal instruments; they describe a complex of social practices (Williams 1991). If those social practices are absent, the legal enunciation of rights is not simply empty, but is an active distortion.

Citizenship is not simply a legal category, but the law is one way of ascertaining the status of a given individual or group of persons. Laws embody (always imperfectly) dominant understandings concerning social goods and communal identity. In Rogers Smith's words (1997, 31), citizenship laws "literally constitute—they create with legal words—a collective civic identity. They proclaim the existence of a political 'people' and designate who those persons are as a people, in ways that often become integral to individuals' senses of personal identity as well" (cf. Curthoys 1993; Stychin 1998). When laws systematically deny some persons the opportunity to share in that communal identity, whether through explicit exclusion from citizenship or through denial of rights and duties considered central to that people's collective identity, we may say that those persons are either "second-class" citizens or are not citizens at all. Thus we may scrutinize laws and policies for the ways in which they enact citizenship, acknowledging some individuals and groups and rejecting others. Full understanding of their impact not only requires that we read the statutes and regulations, but also that we examine patterns of enforcement as well as the concepts and ideologies that dominate public discussion and policy-making. Only a full examination of these elements will determine whether exclusions are incidental, a matter of particular circumstances, or are in fact constitutive of the self-understandings of citizens.

Acknowledgment consists both in legal inclusion and formal rights and in active acknowledgment of individuals and groups as part of the polity. Indeed, we will see that hostility toward sexual minorities is often expressed by asserting their already-equal status; the claim that American lesbians and gays already enjoy full civil and political rights is often used to argue against more specific protections against discrimination. Here a recognition of the presence and legal status of gays and lesbians in fact is an avoidance of acknowledgment, as the grudging assertion of equality is used to harden hearts against them.

Marginal Citizens

Examination of public policy, law, and law enforcement in the United States demonstrates the ambiguous citizen status of sexual minorities. Few states have laws that explicitly penalize lesbians, gays, bisexuals, or transgendered (LBGT) people. They are not barred from civil service positions or elective office (although the Senate's eighteen-month refusal to approve James Hormel as Ambassador to Luxembourg, ended in June 1999 only by a presidential appointment during recess, comes close). No laws exist to pardon violence or fraud against them. They are not quarantined or differentially taxed (unless we include the penalties of exclusion from marriage). By most liberal definitions and understandings, lesbian or gay individuals in the United States enjoy full citizenship rights. This does not mean that no stigma is attached to sexual difference; it simply means that political membership does not require the elimination of all stigma.

When we expand our understanding of citizenship to include acknowledgment and inclusion in the national political imaginary, however, a different picture emerges. At both the legal and cultural levels, gays and lesbians are barred from full membership in the American polity. This is evident in the overt exclusion of "homosexuals" from the military and in immigration law; in sodomy laws; in legal interpretation that disallows same-sex marriage and the recent rise of explicit legal bans; and in the public toleration of discrimination and violence (Amnesty International USA 1994; Comstock 1991; Herman and Stychin 1995; Luibheid 1995; Rimmerman 1996; Wolinsky and Sherrill 1993). These are not the sole indicators of membership, but they are among the most salient and currently contested.

Scholars have recently shown how various New Right groups wrestle with ambivalence between suspicion of the state and desire to use political power to construct a Christian state (Herman 1997; Smith 1994b). For these groups, lesbigay persons are a threat to the integrity and health of the state. Metaphors of invasion, disease, degeneracy, and contamination are central to their rhetoric (Watney 1996). Because the acknowledgment of citizenship requires both "social recognition and legal support" (Kaplan 1997, 208), questions of public framing and support are as relevant to the question of citizenship as the letter of the law. When the law is expressly framed to exclude a group from recognition and participation in a central social institution, that group is being denied both legal rights and political membership.

For example, the U.S. military accepts the identity category of "homosexual" and uses it to bar membership to a distinct population. The military no longer claims that homosexuals are bad soldiers or security risks; several studies conducted between 1957 and 1993 have put the lie to this belief (Crittenden 1957; General Accounting Office 1992,

1993; RAND 1993). Instead, the 1993 congressional hearings relied almost exclusively upon the discomfort of heterosexual troops. Tours of submarines were calculated to evoke heterosexual fears of sharing tight quarters with (presumably predatory) gay men, and military fathers testified that they would ban their gay sons out of fear for their sons' lives.

The idea that the rights and membership of the minority should be enforced even when it makes the majority uncomfortable was largely absent from public testimony and debate. This absence was not due to argument (arguments, indeed, would have made it present) but to presumption and privilege. In order to carry the day, the presumption must conform with pre-existing stigma or exclusion that marks the targeted group as not part of "us," but a "them" to be managed by us. This presumption operated in 1948 when Congress held hearings on ending racial segregation in the armed forces, but it was noticed and challenged (Bianco 1996). Were this rationale used to exclude racial or religious minorities today, it would be seen as patently discriminatory. When used against women, it has become a hotly contested argument for precisely the same reason (Benecke and Dodge 1996; Katzenstein 1996). The argument presumes that the fears of the majority are a legitimate basis for exclusion; the success of such arguments has everything to do with the perception of the worth and importance of the group being excluded. As the status of groups improves, such arguments are less successful precisely because they presuppose the marginalization of the groups they target. Thus the debate over the military, as much as the policy itself, manifested a lack of acknowledgment.

The result of the controversy was a new policy that did not bar homosexuals but instituted a ban on "homosexual conduct" (including speech). This result has proven unsatisfactory. The attempts to distinguish "status" from "conduct" have only muddied the waters on this issue. The courts have not been able to reach agreement on either the nature or the validity of the distinction (Pacelle 1996). Such a distinction reinstates the demand for homosexual celibacy and the closet because it has little applicability in actual life. For the military, homosexual status is constituted by the desire to perform acts; these acts are not only sexual, but sexual acts are central. Banning "homosexual behavior" singles out certain acts that are central to community membership and acknowledgment, including discussion of one's daily life with one's colleagues. "Status" is protected, but the actual living of that status is banned. Both the old and the new policies force some individuals to choose between military duty and personal fulfillment in a way unthinkable for the heterosexual majority. This gap between what seems an acceptable limitation on the lives of some and what would be seen as unconstitutional and invidious for the majority betrays the absence of acknowledgment.

Laws that ban same-sex marriage and sexual activity present a different, but related, set of issues than those raised by military service. If the military case focuses directly on a population ("homosexuals"), marriage laws appear to address an activity, "same-sex marriage," that might be engaged in by anyone. Indeed, in *Baehr v. Lewin,* the Hawai'i case that touched off a national firestorm by suggesting that bans on same-sex marriage might constitute discrimination on the basis of sex (not sexual orientation), the court distinguished between "homosexual" marriage (not a right) and "same-sex marriage" (potentially a fundamental right). Thus, the Hawai'i Supreme Court did not endorse "marriage for homosexuals," but the choice of marriage partner for anyone, of any orientation or preference. Nonetheless, the ban amounts to a denial of acknowledgment of the circumstances of lesbian and gay life. Lesbians and gays grow up in the midst of larger social understandings of the purpose and goals of human life, and these include publicly recognized committed relationships. Denial to some of such a publicly valorized, state-sanctioned relation is tantamount to excluding those persons from full membership. The failure to recognize the ways in which these laws bar intimacy from the lives of gay men and lesbians is the result of, as well as continuing mechanism for, the deprivation of membership in the political community.

In fact, the situation is more stark than this. Far from using putatively egalitarian arguments, opponents explicitly link same-sex marriage to homosexuality, which in turn is figured as sexual chaos. The refusal of acknowledgment is not implicit or denied, but is avowed.

Marriage and sodomy laws present a challenging case for theorists of citizenship. It might be claimed that insofar as such laws affect our private lives rather than our political participation, they are irrelevant to citizenship. This argument can be rooted in either an Aristotelian vision of citizenship and a corresponding public/private split, or in a modern separation between public and private. Such arguments are not obviously wrong, and in fact the division between public and private has for years been a staple of arguments against anti-sodomy laws. Certainly privacy is a fundamental prerequisite for the formation and maintenance of autonomous selves. Privacy is not, however, simply a matter for pre-social individuals being left alone; as Morris Kaplan (1997, 207) explains, "even the most intimate associations between individuals are situated within a matrix of social relations and legal arrangements that both constrain and support them." The "private" is not simply opposed to "the public," but is the creature of social and political arrangements that foster certain zones and forms of privacy and overlook others.

This is especially true in the case of marriage. Arguments based on privacy alone overlook the substantial documentation and argument concerning the "public" nature of marriage and the family. Throughout recorded history states have treated the regulation of marriage and family as one of their central functions, and contemporary theorists have elaborated upon this concern (Elshtain 1982; Okin 1989; Pateman 1988; Peterson and Parisi 1997). Modern states have sustained this role, expanding from regulation of property (including women and children) to concerns for child welfare, education, public morals, and health, often figured explicitly as national concerns (Mosse 1985) The recent flurry of state and national legislation designed to ward off the possibility of same-sex marriage, and the public rhetoric of "defense" surrounding such legislation, makes abundantly clear that for many Americans marriage is not in fact simply a "private" matter but is rather a private matter between two individuals who fit the publicly sanctioned requirements. The establishment of the criteria for marriage, however, is an important and widely accepted state function. To the extent that the state withholds acknowledgment of lesbian and gay relationships, it actively discriminates against a portion of its population.

Equal citizenship requires equal treatment by political authorities and by other citizens. In a society where marriage is a state function, regulated by the state and given force through policies concerning taxes, rights, and benefits, it is clear that the intimacy of marriage occurs within a zone created and regulated by the state. In such a society, arguments that marriage is a "private" matter rather than an issue of public concern are disingenuous at best. The recent controversies over marriage make clear that exclusion from marriage is for many opponents an integral part of a larger desire to withhold acknowledgment of LGBT persons.

The problem of violence against gays and lesbians is perhaps the clearest manifestation of the denial of citizenship. Not only are they the target of the greatest number of hate crimes in the United States; not only is violence against them not redressed by the police or the courts; the police are among the most notorious and most vicious perpetrators of anti-gay violence and abuse (Comstock 1991; Herek and Berrill 1992). The most minimal elements of legal or "negative" citizenship, in which citizens trade obedience to the laws in exchange for protection, are thus denied to legal citizens who fail to meet the sexual/gendered requirements for effective membership. Failure to arrest and prosecute those who prey upon gays and lesbians is thus a prima facie denial of membership. The low percentage of attacks reported is based in gay and lesbian people's awareness that their membership is subject to erasure by homophobic public officials, employers, and neighbors. The stigma of homosexuality is often considered to be a greater burden than the absence of redress for assault, and for good reason; many people lose their jobs, housing, or community prestige once an attack discloses their sexual orientation (Herek and Berrill 1992).

The legitimacy of the principle of equal protection in these cases has been clear enough for some municipal, state, and national officials to work with gay and lesbian activists to curb violence (Dufour 1995; Vaid 1995). Nonetheless, hatred of homosexuals remains strong enough for many legislators and citizens to refuse to endorse equal protection. The rejection of hate-crimes legislation that includes sexual orientation is only one example of this. The fact that some legislators have accepted such legislation until sexual orientation is included tells us much about which populations are considered worthy of state protection and which are considered legitimately excluded. Even more telling is the silence of public figures when asked to condemn violence against lesbians and gays. In the light of active campaigns of vilification engaged in by Christian Right organizations (Herman 1997), the insistence that lesbians and gays have equal rights in the United States rings hollow.

Protection against violence is the most minimal guarantee required not only for citizenship, but for a legitimate state. Without this guarantee, individuals have no reason to believe themselves within civil society at all. This is true not only in a social contractarian view of the state, but in any community. The fundamental requirement of any political community is sufficient common purpose and solidarity among members to value and protect one another, whether directly or through a state apparatus. When some are denied this solidarity, they are in effect expelled from the political community. Their physical and verbal presence does not make them members.

The cases of the military, marriage, and violence raise important questions concerning civil rights. Framed in that context, each is relevant for the legal understanding of citizens as persons possessed of the rights conferred upon citizens within a polity. This is an important element of citizenship, but it is not the sum of such membership. Civil rights speak to what is due to a citizen, and thus their denial suggests a refusal of citizenship. However, having civil rights is not all there is to citizenship. The primary question of recognition and acknowledgment is not addressed solely through the laws, but also through the public and intimate fora in which we make our common lives.

Lesbigay people confront legal exclusions and failures of enforcement within an environment that makes those exclusions and failures less socially stigmatized than their victims. Legislators who might sympathize with and support proponents of equality find themselves constantly under pressure not to look like "supporters" of homosexuality; rarely is it more costly to a legislator to deny equality than to support it (Haider-Markel and Meier 1996). Exclusions are not only denials of civil rights, but reflect and reinforce social stigmatization that limits political participation. Political activity is "symbolic" as well as "substantive" (Edelman 1964), both for actors initiating a policy change and for their opponents, and primary among the symbolic goals of politics are recognition and legitimation (Hertzog 1996, 34–35). Political activity that challenges exclusions may be seen as the emergence of citizenship among people slated for invisibility, but such citizenship also requires a measure of acknowledgment from others.

Many might conclude from the above that lesbians and gays are not citizens of the United States in either the civil or political senses of that word. Although they are subject to the laws, they are not afforded their protection. They are explicitly excluded from two central institutions of social membership in modern societies, in the case of the military by the designation of a stigmatized identity ("homosexuals"), and in the case of marriage by the refusal to afford satisfying access to a social practice that is widely seen as part of adult fulfillment. Nonetheless, many who would grant that gays and lesbians are excluded in the ways I have described might still balk at the claim that they are not citizens. Homosexuality is not a bar to participation; indeed, the Supreme Court's 1996 decision in *Romer v. Evans*, in which Colorado's ban on sexual orientation anti-discrimination laws was held to be unconstitutional, hinged precisely on the need to protect the right to participate in the political process. The increased social visibility and equality of sexual minorities is directly responsible for current efforts to contain and subjugate them. Many groups that are marginalized or dominated are nonetheless understood as citizens.

Traditionally, such dilemmas have been addressed through the category of "second-class citizen." As Rogers Smith (1997, 256) documents, U.S. courts in the past accepted the idea that "citizenship had multiple classes, with only the most fortunate or worthy receiving full political privileges." Racial, gender, and other hierarchies thus have been maintained even in regimes formally adhering to liberal democratic notions of citizenship. Nor is this phenomenon solely a relic of our past: "Many Americans today still find a body of civic laws aimed at realizing liberal egalitarian principles unacceptable—some because those principles seem too limited in their consequences, many more because they are perceived as threatening the social and cultural order, however hierarchical, which these citizens feel to be essential to their secure possession of meaningful social identities" (Smith 1989, 289).

The phrase "second-class citizen" has been rhetorically effective both because it represents the duality of legal equality and daily marginalization and because it challenges the universalist ideals of liberal regimes. The belief that the United States is and should be a classless society makes the language of second-class citizenship a potent resource for argument; indeed, the majority opinion in *Romer v. Evans* quoted Justice Harlan's famous statement that "the Constitution neither knows nor tolerates classes among citizens."

The resonance of second-class citizenship should not, however, be allowed to obscure its limitations. "Second-class" status is indeed a status, a position within a polity. It may be a subordinate, marginal position, but it offers a recognition of sorts. For example, women may accurately be described as second-class citizens who are moving toward full citizenship. Women historically have not been excluded from the polity, but have been included in subordinate roles. Arguments against fuller equality have often drawn on the idea that women have a unique place of honor and importance in the home. This view is substantively different from the sorts of arguments offered for the exclusion of non-heterosexuals. The position of opponents of lesbigay military inclusion and same-sex marriage has been justified not by claiming that inclusion is already adequate, but rather by actively stigmatizing the target population as unfit and dangerous. Rather than rationalizing a valuable but subordinate role, as have opponents of gender equality, those advancing anti-gay arguments consistently figure non-heterosexuals as alien and dangerous to "the community" (Bianco 1996; Herman 1997; Watney 1996). This is a curious sort of visibility, one aptly named by Maria Lugones and Elizabeth Spelman (1983) as "cultural imperialism." As they describe it, cultural imperialism consists in the simultaneous visibility of stereotypical presentations of a group with the invisibility of individuals, especially as they fail to conform to the stereotype. Thus, as Iris Marion Young (1990, 60) puts it, "cultural imperialism involves the paradox of experiencing oneself as invisible at the same time that one is marked out as different."

Simon Watney (1996) details this process of exclusion in his treatment of media coverage of AIDS. Watney demonstrates the ways in which the association between AIDS and gay men shaded both media treatment and governmental policy. For both, as he puts it, "the very notion of 'the general public' is massively heterosexualized" (29) and gays are figured as Other, either outside the body politic threatening to invade it, or insidious insiders threatening internal degeneration. The concern to differentiate "innocent victims" (i.e., heterosexual, non–drug users) from other persons with AIDS, present in both the American and the British press throughout the 1980s and 1990s, reinforces the idea that gays deserve to die, that they are in Watney's words "a disposable population" (133). Cathy Cohen's research (1999) into AIDS politics in the African-American community, where AIDS service organizations do not include gay men on their boards or in their service mission, once again bears this out.

Carlos Forment (1995) has recently used the formulation of second-class citizenship to refer to people who, whether on the basis of gender, sexuality, religion, race, national origin, or ethnicity, "have been driven by the discriminatory practices of their compatriots to occupy marginal positions in the 'central institutions' of their own homeland" (316). He contrasts the "relatively stable and secure" legal status of such citizens with their experiences of "social degradation" and "the absence of full political equality and social inclusion" (ibid.). Forment's description speaks to the experience of many diverse groups. Rather than focus narrowly on legal categories of privilege and responsibility, Forment aims as well to integrate economic, cultural, and social status into the understanding of citizenship. Rather than a linear hierarchy of classes, citizenship presents itself in a relation of core and peripheries, peripheries which are not equivalent to one another but manifest their own unique, if similar and sometimes related, situations.

Forment locates second-class citizens within a larger category he labels "peripheral peoples," whose groups are significantly different from one another yet also share commonalities. He includes sexual minorities in his list of peripheral peoples, but his analysis fundamentally rests on the experience of racial and national minorities. This is a significant gap. The discourses that produce and justify the exclusion of sexual minorities resemble those used to exclude other groups (indeed, at points such as the military debate they are virtually indistinguishable), but are also distinct. Anti-gay stigma involves a revulsion that is rationalized by appeals to the immoral nature of homosexual desire. That is, to be queer is to be perverted. This understanding has been justified through many discourses in modernity. The Christian citation of Leviticus 20:13 and St. Paul's prohibitions in Romans as authority for such a position is in fact more recent, and more contentious, than contemporary readings would suggest. John Boswell (1980, 1994) has documented the changing position of the Christian Church toward homosexual activity, including same-sex marriage, locating a clear shift from approval or indifference to sanction only in the twelfth century. Modern translations, combined with literalist readings of the Bible, have made seemingly self-evident a stricture that in fact developed contingently over centuries. The medical discourse of homosexuality, originating in the nineteenth century, presented same-sex desire as symptomatic of larger personality (mal) formations. In tandem with the larger nineteenth-century discourse of degeneration and decadence, the new class of persons marked by homosexuality became emblematic of modern urban decadence (Gilman 1985, 1991; Mosse 1985). In this discourse the otherness of homosexuals was dramatically similar to that of Jews (Arendt 1966, 80ff.); both were presented as "types," different from and threatening to the healthy social body. Homosexuals were simultaneously figured as inherently different from heterosexuals and yet seductive, with the possibility of contaminating heterosexuals ("recruitment," in today's language). Contemporary anti-gay sentiment draws on both these discourses for inspiration and justification; indeed, they are so pervasive as to be "common sense" to many. Efforts by racial minorities to prove their responsible membership in political society and assumption of authority have almost universally included condemnation of homosexuality as a sign of decadence. In communist countries homosexuality has been seen as a "bourgeois deviation"; in capitalist zones it has been linked to communism and other threats to national integrity; and in anti-colonial and postcolonial struggles it is demonized as a perversion of the colonizers (Alexander 1991; D'Emilio 1983; Lumsden 1996; Trujillo 1991; Young 1981).

As a system of hierarchy, heterosexism also reverses the relation between ascription and individual choice that prevails in most other systems of domination. Justifications for the oppression of women, for instance, have treated the differences between men and women as immutable facts of nature. Tampering with these relations will bring social disaster, as society is founded on this natural difference. Opponents have argued that many differences are the result of practices, such as mother-only child rearing, that produce certain sorts of people. Likewise, arguments for racial equality in a liberal framework generally argue for the essential sameness of people across groups while opponents appeal to something basic and immutable. In contrast, public discourse about homosexuality finds advocates of equality arguing for immutablity and opponents demanding that sexual orientation is a matter of behavior that can and must be controlled (Currah 1996). The "immutable difference" of homosexuality is then, ironically enough, figured by advocates of equality as a basic difference that has no public consequences, while opponents present it as a contingent difference with the capacity to destroy society. This reverse casting may be understood as the particular dilemma of sexual strangers.

Sexual Strangers

In *Modernity and Ambivalence* Zygmunt Bauman (1991) describes modernity as a regime uniquely devoted to order and binary classification. These goals have in turn generated intense antagonism toward those who do not fit within binaries. The primary binary that Bauman focuses on is that between friends and enemies. While "friends and enemies stand in opposition to each other" (53), this antagonism can never contain the whole social world. Any binary scheme generates "undecidables," and the friend/enemy antagonism is no exception. The social undecidable generated by the friend/enemy binary is the stranger. The particular provocation of the stranger is that strangers are neighbors, but "they are not like 'us'" (Beck 1996, 382). Strangers are not like enemies, who are clearly other; they both are and are not "us." Indeed, "enemies themselves are, to put it sharply, in a certain respect less threatening than strangers because they obey the established order of the stereotypes of self and other" (384). Strangers disrupt seemingly natural boundaries and borders. They thus present a challenge to identities, including national identities. The stranger "refuses to remain confined to the 'far away' land or go away from our own and hence a priori defies the easy expedient of spatial or temporal segregation" (Bauman 1991, 59). Strangers seem to be both friends and enemies, on the one hand making their way "into the life-world uninvited, thereby casting me on the receiving side of his initiative, making me into the object of action of which he is the subject" and on the other hand claiming "a right to be an object of responsibility" (ibid.). The stranger is "physically close while remaining spiritually remote," disrupting the taken-for-grantedness of home and community (60). Indeed, Bauman suggests that the stranger "saps social life itself" in that s/he makes it impossible to be secure in the "within" of one's own (55). Not simply "outside," strangers are thus not just determined by the fact that they are demarcated from others; they are determined much more by the fact that they undermine and crack open from inside all polar categories of social order. Strangers are neither enemies nor friends, neither natives nor foreigners; they are near and not near, far, yet here; they are neighbors, who would be closed off by neighbors as non-neighbors (Beck 1996, 385). They are the "inappropriate other" who simultaneously engages in "at least two gestures: that of affirming 'I am like you' while persisting in her difference and that of reminding 'I am different' while unsettling every definition of otherness arrived at" (Trinh 1990, 375).

Bauman traces the consequences of strangeness for Jews in modernity, through successive attempts to assimilate or reject assimilation, to claim participation in a universal humanity or to celebrate a distinctive Jewish identity, as liberal regimes confront their own cultural presumptions. Sexual minorities are also usefully understood as strangers. Indeed, their strangeness is more intense even than that of Jews. Gays and lesbians do not constitute a population with fixed territory or a unified national, ethnic, or racial history that clearly distinguishes them from their neighbors. Homosexual desire and activity occur across and within cultures, nations, and families, and the recent formation of a homosexual identity has not eliminated that fact. Gays and lesbians do not have a "home" to return to, either in territorial/historical terms or in the sense of present-day enclaves; most gays and lesbians live amidst their heterosexual families and neighbors without the promise even of a local community center to find affirmation and support. Most grow up convinced that they are "the only one" in their communities. Urban centers ameliorate this situation for those with the resources and desire to relocate, but such relocation involves a separation from, and often a rejection of, their community of birth. Those who do not want to live in cities, or who cannot so choose, often live their lives in isolation. Even those who create a home or a common culture are in a situation drastically different from that faced by racial, ethnic, or national groups; such cultures and homes are created as adults, after the experience of isolation and rejection from one's family and community.

Partly as a result of this situation of dispersion and lack of history, lesbians and gays present their neighbors with a fundamental strangeness. This strangeness, in turn, is "frightening and enticing" (Beck 1996, 385). The fears of "recruitment" and "seduction" so prevalent in right-wing treatments of homosexuality are not manifestations of something distinctive about homosexuality, or even about homophobia, but rather examples of a general ambivalence about the practices of strangers. As Hannah Arendt noted in *The Origins of Totalitarianism* (1966), the fears concerning Jews closely parallelled those concerning homosexuals, as both became "types" in the nineteenth century. Both became figures of corruption and urban decadence, simultaneously repellent and somehow irresistible.

This dynamic of attraction and repulsion illuminates the centrality of abjection in strangeness. The abject, as Julia Kristeva (1982, 4) describes it, is not lack or opposition, but "the in-between, the ambiguous, the composite"; the abject is "something rejected from which one does not part." Neither acceptable nor removable, the abject persists within a culture or a psyche that seems to expel it. This liminal status creates a unique sort of corruption. In contrast to the criminal or the enemy, whose opposition to the order is well-defined, the abject is "immoral, sinister, scheming, and shady: a terror that dissembles, a hatred that smiles, a passion that uses the body for barter instead of inflaming it, a debtor who sells you up, a friend who stabs you . . . " (ibid.). Many subaltern peoples have been described in exactly these terms, the more so as they become more intimately connected to the dominant culture. Instead of being simply different, or simply objects for the dominant gaze, such subalterns approach the condition of being objects who demand subject status. As they do, the gap between intragroup "hidden transcripts" (Scott 1990) and dominant narratives becomes visible to the dominant group. Dominant group members come to suspect or to know that the presentation of self made to them is not the only presentation made by subalterns, and so the theme of betrayal and cunning, rather than outright antagonism, develops. Strangers are not just "not like us," as enemies are, but may "pretend" to be like us. In fact, the more the stranger attempts to become "like us" the more threatening s/he becomes, and the greater the potential for betrayal as relevant boundaries are seemingly crossed. At the same time, the stranger's attempts to become "like us" reaffirm the superiority of the dominant group: they are a "recognition of the extant hierarchy, its legitimacy, and above all its immutability" (Bauman 1991, 105). The stranger's attempts to fit in reinforce her status as "a shoddy counterfeit" (71), as we see in the Right's insistence on the phrase "pretended marriages" for same-sex unions.

The stranger may engage in several strategies in response to exclusion. The most favored strategy in liberal regimes is assimilation, but it is not the only one. Strangers may, and as we will see often do, "retreat into strangerhood" in order to find solidarity and confidence. Alternatively, they may attempt to subvert the hierarchies of the hegemonic order, pointing out the gaps and contradictions in that order (e.g., Berlant 1997; Butler 1991), thus removing the privilege of innocence from the dominant group. In our time, if assimilation is the favored strategy of mainstream groups such as the Human Rights Campaign and the National Gay and Lesbian Task Force, the latter strategies have been adopted by those calling themselves "queer." Subsequent chapters will consider these strategies in turn. They are divided by understandings of personal and sexual identity, democratic politics, and desired goals, but they are united in their forced confrontation of their position as strangers.

Confronting the strangeness of sexual minorities inevitably turns us back toward a reconsideration of the American polity as a whole. Is the United States the land defined by the ideals of liberal democracy or liberal republicanism, or is it the land of Christian manifest destiny? Or is it, as Rogers Smith (1997) has persuasively argued, a "fierce new world" shaped in turn by liberal, republican, and "inegalitarian ascriptivist" ideologies? To the extent that mainstream assimilationist strategies are forced to speak the language of liberal republicanism, they cannot confront other elements that are crucial to contemporary American civic identity. The imperative of state-building in modernity relies on the creation of a people and a civic identity, not merely legislation of principles of justice. These identities, and the "civic myths" that explain their origins and boundaries (33), are necessarily exclusive. The particular exclusions that are taken to be crucial help to define the group. Liberal principles alone cannot do the work of state-building and civic identity. Neither can civic myths and identities be easily or quickly transformed to include those previously marked "other." Thus the road to queer citizenship, if such be possible, must take us from strangeness through the construction of polity that creates it.

Is the Body Politic Heterosexual?

It is not yet fully clear just how entrenched or basic the strangeness of homosexuality is or how deep the exclusion of sexual minorities runs. Is it, as liberals have said in the past of sexism and racism, a breach of modern ideals? Or is it rather constitutive of the modern United States, and perhaps of modern states in general? The connection between hetero-sexism as a regime and modern citizenship is a new terrain beginning to be explored (Peterson 1999; Stychin 1998); as it is, we find that Carole Pateman's (1988) observations on the constitutive role of women's sub-ordination in liberal regimes have a corollary in the exclusion of overt same-sex desire. Without confronting this connection, political drives for equality will be palliative at best.

One might argue that the exclusions detailed earlier are not central to the meaning of citizenship in the modern United States, but are the results of prejudice that can and will be overcome. Another possible response is that the exclusions are justifiable and even important, but nonetheless are not relevant to our understandings of citizenship. Thus, one might either approve or disapprove of the exclusion of les-bigay persons from central social institutions while denying that such exclusions are important for understanding the contemporary United States.

There are several avenues through which one might make the case for heterosexuality's constitutive role in contemporary U.S. citizenship. The first, prima facie, approach draws on evident exclusions such as marriage and the military to demonstrate the increasingly systematic and conscious nature of exclusion. These will be explored at greater length in later chapters. This demonstration can be supplemented by the rhetoric of the opponents of homosexuality, who have argued that the state has an interest both in promoting heterosexual marriage and discouraging other forms of affiliation and in excluding from the mili-tary those it deems detrimental to unit cohesion. For many such oppo-nents, the state can and should claim an interest in reproduction and child-rearing, and limitation of marriage to different-sex couples fur-thers this interest. Thus, such thinkers might very well agree that the modern state is, or should be, heterosexual.

This argument, however, runs afoul of both liberal ideals and his-tory. Although the early Protestant attitude toward marriage and sexu-ality focused on the family and reproduction, the consensus that marriage was intended for and justified only by reproduction was short-lived (D'Emilio and Freedman 1988, ch. 1). Both in popular culture and, eventually, in law, marriage came to be seen as a union of souls bound in love. Contemporary usages of this argument have the persistent shortcoming, furthermore, of covering too much territory in their mandate. If marriage is legitimately regulated because of a state interest in reproduction, what should be the state's position toward childless marriages? Should marriages without children be deemed legally non-binding? Surely that is not the current position of law or policy; marriage is recognized whether one has children or not. As long as this remains the case, the argument by procreation will fail. That argument is also complicated by the many lesbigay families that include children. If procreation and child-rearing were the sole state interests in marriage, then surely such families would be recognized as legitimate units equal to heterosexual unions. Although modern states have increasingly interested themselves in the reproduction and health of the body politic (Foucault 1978), their concern has not been limited to reproduction.

Laws against sodomy, or against same-sex intimacy, are also not enough to establish heterosexuality as constitutive of a regime. Such laws ban acts that are central to human fulfillment for many, and I take them to be unjust. The question of sexual regimes, however, goes beyond such laws. In order to establish that heterosexuality is constitutive of modern citizenship, we must examine the ways in which heterosexuality is presumed as well as the means by which lesbigay people are excluded because of their sexual orientation. The very notion of homosexuality as a condition, and of heterosexuality as its opposite, is the product of medical/social regimes that distinguished themselves by their concern not only for reproduction but also for the "social hygiene" of their populations. It is in this history that we should look for the heterosexual regime and its conception of citizenship.

The history of the military ban provides one example of how new social categories come to inflect citizenship. Prior to World War I, the military had no laws against homosexuality. The Articles of War included sodomy as a crime only in 1919. Such laws barred particular acts, but they did not go so far as to exclude classes of people on the basis of suspected or declared sexual orientation. Between the wars, a growing number of psychiatrists began to warn that "homosexualists" could not be effective fighters and that they would constitute a danger to other soldiers (Shilts 1993, 15). Such warnings relied upon the new construction of "the homosexual" as a discrete type, different in all ways from and dangerous to the majority population, a construction that had already gained force in civilian society (Arendt 1966; Foucault 1978). Civil Service regulations were amended to bar homosexuals from the civil service, and the Senate in 1950 produced a cautionary report on the presence of "sex perverts" in the government (Blasius and Phelan 1997). Although Civil Service regulations were eventually changed, the military ban continues today.

Social policy also reflects the growing heterosexualization of the citizen. The systematic privileging of marriage in tax policy and legal recognition has heightened the exclusion of those who are denied the opportunity to marry. While marriage has never been a fully private matter in the United States but has always carried legal implications for property and income rights, the growth of the welfare state (including welfare in the form of tax breaks, availability of credit and insurance, etc.) has been explicitly linked to the mandate to foster heterosexual family units. The recent Defense of Marriage Act is only the most explicit statement of this mandate.

It is not surprising that the sexualization of the citizen has not been a topic for public debate. Within a heterosexual world, heterosexuality is presumed; just as white is a default category among whites, seemingly "un-raced" or neutral, heterosexuality is a position that is so unremarkable among heterosexuals that it becomes invisible as a structure. Thus many heterosexuals express a certain tolerance for homosexuals, but object to "flaunting it," arguing that they do not make public display and issue of their own sexuality. In fact, however, every marriage ceremony, every coffee-break discussion, every induction exam is a site for heterosexual display.

Current debates over inclusion have not only foregrounded the ways in which heterosexuality is presumed by political communities in the United States; they have also served as locations for the progressively more self-conscious articulation of heterosexual identity and the intensification of the heterosexual body politic. As they have done so, they have transformed the identities and positions of sexual minorities in general, and homosexuals in particular, from fully excluded individuals, seen only as enemies when seen at all, to strangers at home. The stranger, as much or perhaps more than the enemy, shows the contours and depths of liberal regimes. As sexual strangers, sexual minorities both highlight the heterosexuality of the U.S. body politic and challenge that construction. This is their dilemma and their potential.

Structures of Strangeness
Bodies, Passions, and Citizenship

nderstanding strangeness requires an examination of the regime that creates it. This is especially the case where the exclusion is so unevenly distributed as it is at present in the United States. The United States is not one community, not one culture, but a multiplicity of cultural, economic, legal, and political sites held together by a combination of force, history, and continually created national identity. We may, then, expect to see that exclusions at certain points coexist with cautious inclusions at some other sites and comfortable equality at yet others. Each exclusion rests on larger ideas about the relations between public and private, citizen and family member, sexual discipline and political order.

The debates over military inclusion and same-sex marriage, both within lesbian and gay communities and in the general U.S. population, highlight two of the few explicit legal exclusions from widely recognized political and civil aspects of citizenship. This exclusion is especially notable because military service has for so many centuries in so many cultures been considered a central element of citizenship, thus affording us greater insight into the relations among citizenship, masculinity, and military service, while marriage and family have been viewed as the quintessentially "feminine sphere." It also reveals glimpses of the ways in which failures of acknowledgment leave a group of nominally equal citizens subject to the deliberations and decisions of others who see them as a problem rather than as members of society.

The battle for inclusion in the military has documented the extent to which military service continues to be seen as the ultimate act of citizenship. The public testimony of many soldiers has focused on their desire to "serve their country," with no examination of the assumption that this is the best, or the only, way to serve (Cammermeyer 1994; Humphrey 1990; Steffan 1992). "Internal" community newspapers, however, have continued a (somewhat muted) debate about the military (e.g., Tatchell 1995). The controversy among gays and lesbians has reprised many feminist debates about the military (Elshtain and Tobias 1990; Enloe 1993; Katzenstein 1996; Stiehm 1989). Many are split between their desire to be included, or at least not rejected, and their acknowledgment of feminist critiques of the military. Likewise, critical debates about marriage and family, once a staple of LGB communities, have become muted in the 1990s (although see Lehr 1999 and Warner 1999 for important exceptions).

The rationale for the bans functions as a mirror for conceptions of citizenship and sexuality. In the contemporary United States, masculinity has been constructed as predation on other, more "feminine" bodies (D'Amico 1996). Homosexual desire on the part of men, then, can only be perceived as potential aggression against other men. Gay men are stigmatized as effeminate, but they are also feared as hypermasculine, examples of the chaotic desires of men unrestrained by women (Herman 1997, 76). The complex of understandings that link masculinity to military service and define such service as the quintessence of citizenship (see, e.g., Enloe 1990), ensure that gay men and all women are unfit for membership. We must therefore consider to what extent masculinity is required for citizenship, and what sort of masculinity is considered appropriate. Likewise, treatment of the family highlights the exclusions and subordinations within citizenship that are responsible not for the oppression of women but for the creation of sexual strangers.

Exclusion is not only a matter of simple exclusion or boundary-drawing, however. As the military case shows perhaps better than any other, the modern construction of masculine bodies is profoundly threatened by homosexuality; indeed, the masculinity of male soldiers is explicitly contrasted to stereotypes of homosexuality as well as femininity. This was evident in the "shower question" (and its companion, the bunk-space question) that emerged in the 1993 congressional hearings. It has been profoundly important as well for AIDS policy. The citizenship of sexual minorities has been challenged, even to the point of suggesting that they be quarantined or identified by tattoos. If "the body in modern social systems has become 'the principal field of political and cultural activity'" (Schilling 1993, quoting Turner 1992), AIDS has become the most dominant site for expressing fears about bodies and, for many, homosexuality has come to be equated with AIDS.

The threat to the phallic body operates not only in physically intimate spaces but also in the body politic. Metaphors of the body have operated throughout European and American history to explain and justify particular regimes; in an interplay of micro/macro relations, "images of the body act as diagrams of social order" while "particular bodies live out ideas of social order in the flesh." Through this interplay "a shared set of corporeal metaphors are drawn upon to imagine the conditions of unity and integrity for both the social field ad the particular body, and in the process to reconcile the one to the other" (Waldby 1996, 89).

In this chapter I examine relations among gender, citizenship, and political institutions in the United States. I argue that objections to the equal citizenship of lesbians, gays, bisexuals, and transgendered people are constituted and articulated through concerns for the integrity of the heterosexual masculine individual, the heterosexual family, and the body politic. Understandings of citizenship have always been dependent upon particular notions of what sort of bodily integrity is needed and how that integrity is maintained; these notions operate at the level of both the individual citizen body and the body politic. Conceptions of the citizen body and the body politic vary across nation-states, even across Anglophone countries (Stychin 1998). These conceptions are in turn articulated with notions of kinship, public and private, and civil rights in ways that systematically exclude sexual minorities from the legal and cultural landscapes. (I discuss these notions and conflicts concerning them in Chapter 3). The United States presents perhaps the most extreme version of the general phenomena I will discuss; I must wait for others to nuance this portrait across other terrains. Queer/ed citizenship requires not only inclusion into existing frameworks but full-scale refiguring of the body politic. Liberal strategies will fail as long as the phallic body remains untouched.

Citizen Bodies

Cultural conceptions of bodies have been among the major vehicles of masculinism in the West. Understandings of the required features of the citizen's body, imbricated with cultural conceptions about various sorts of bodies, have worked to exclude from citizenship the majority of the population of most Western nations. Through metaphors of the body politic, cultural conceptions about physical bodies migrate as well into rhetorics about and policies of nation-states. These rhetorics express and construct new opportunities and threats to political units, including states, nations, and social movements. The trope of the body structures concerns for (among others) integration, boundaries, power, autonomy, freedom, and order. Thus the idea of the body works both to delineate who shall be a member of the polity and to prescribe the nature of the polity itself.

Some theorists have found the body politic to be a positive and fruitful concept. John O'Neill (1985, 77), for example, argues that the body politic "is the fundamental structure of our political life. It provides the ultimate grounds of appeal in times of institutional crisis, hunger and alienation, when there is need to renew the primary bonds of political authority and social consensus." O'Neill's concern for the rise of technocratic/administrative logics leads him to celebrate "anthropomorphism and familism" as "the root values of political discourse seeking to correct the excesses of neo-individualism and statism" (83). Others, such as Waldby, have pointed out that the other side of the body politic's bonding function is the delegitimation of that which is excluded from current social consensus. The role that O'Neill finds so reassuring is exactly the one that others fear.

Tropes of the body allow for particularly powerful migrations of concerns about gender and sexuality into political discourse (Schatzki and Natter 1996; Waldby 1996). These concerns emerge in foreign policy as well as in legislation on health and welfare, immigration, regulation of media, education, and family policy. Fear of chaos and disorder, of sexual predation, and of the loss of control meet the desire to transgress prohibitions and reach beyond the given meet on the many terrains of political action.

Concern for the intact body politic has, ironically, often been predicated on neglect of the individual body. This neglect is not unique to liberalism or to modernity. Even while planning for the physical fitness of the guardians, Plato dismisses the body as an intrinsically unimportant aspect of human life. Aristotle acknowledges the facts of embodiment, but relegates them to the *oikos*, the sphere of "mere life." For both, the good life focuses not on the body but on the development of intellectual and political virtues. Too much attention to the body is inconsistent with freedom. Christian thinkers continue this disregard, often in quite extreme ways (though of course Luther is an exception). The greatest modern inspiration for communitarianism, G.W.F. Hegel, repeats Aristotle's pattern of attention and dismissal as he finds the family to be the realm of arbitrariness and nature. This is appropriate for women, but "man has his actual substantive life in the state, in learning, and so forth, as well as in labour and struggle with the external world and with himself" (Hegel 1979, 114). The family offers merely an "intuition" of his eventual reconciliation with himself, a reconciliation that must be achieved by transcending the family.

The denigration of the family is part and parcel of the denial of the body in political theory. Or rather, the body that is presented as appropriate for citizenship is a body stripped of its vulnerability to daily events; while capable of dying in battle, the citizen body is otherwise phallic in its invulnerability. It is a body without bodily needs, bodily processes, or bodily decay.

The predominant account of the relation between bodies and citizenship has been produced in feminist theory (Berlant 1997; Bordo 1993; Butler 1990; Carver 1996). This critique has suggested that not only is the body of the citizen normatively male, but also that this maleness makes it invisible in regimes of Western societies. The opposition male/female is linked to mind/body, and citizens as rational beings are construed not only as male, but as characterized only incidentally by bodies though curiously, it is their body that tells us in daily life that they belong to the class of persons for whom bodies are secondary). A variant of this position does not deny that men have bodies, but it denies that they *are* bodies. The contrast between male and female is not between embodied beings and disembodied minds, but rather ranks how much that embodiment affects their lives. Male bodies are containers for minds that guide bodies, while female bodies overwhelm their minds. To be visible as a man, then, is not to be exposed but simply to be present. This is not a simple project of privilege, but requires significant sacrifice and renunciation on the part of dominant men; "the abstraction 'man' acquires an important disciplinary function vis-à-vis men, as well as women" (Carver 1996, 678), and also disciplines white middle-class men on their way to disciplining people of color and workers (Foucault 1978). Thus, not all male bodies count as appropriate citizen bodies; stigmatization and inferiority are marked on the body, as it were, so that disembodiment is not an all-or-nothing proposition but admits of varieties of scale and design. In contemporary Western societies, the embodiment of stigma means that non-white men are more fully embodied than white men and workers are more embodied than middle-class men. Gay men, defined in heterosexual society entirely by their sexuality, are so completely embodied as to threaten civilization itself. Speaking of the development of modern masculinity in the late nineteenth century, R. W. Connell (1987, 196) makes this point by asserting that "hegemonic masculinity was purged in terms of sexuality." Specifically, "the potential for homoerotic pleasure was expelled from the masculine and located in a deviant group, symbolically assimilated to women or to beasts. There was no mirror-type of 'the heterosexual.' Rather, heterosexuality became a required part of manliness."

The normative male body is not simply absent, but is phallic. The phallic body is impermeable, a source but never a receptacle. Such a conception works within a chain of associations that link personal receptivity, vulnerability, fluidity, and disintegration of the self (Irigaray 1985). Thus, as Anthony Easthope (1986, 53) tells us, "the most important meanings that can attach to the idea of the masculine body are unity and permanence." This stability is both physical and mental. Men, guided by inner imperatives and directed by reason, find their goals and their way without deviating. The phallic ideal of the body is also manifested in the masculine denial of physical pain and in the suspicion and disdain shown to men who notice and fashion their bodies. Each of these gendered associations plays off the idea that masculine bodies and minds are fixed, stable, self-maintaining, and invulnerable.

In sharp contrast, feminine bodies are "castrated," incomplete, and vulnerable. Their distance from the signifier of strength and purpose leaves them weak in both body and mind. This is evident in a myriad of daily associations. Note, for example, the popular saying that changing one's mind is "a woman's prerogative" but not a man's. Women are fickle, both in thoughts and desires, and must be tolerated by men (who of course know their own minds and so do not change). This is consistent with women's fuller embodiment and their consequent susceptibility to the change that is part of the phenomenal world.

This difference in bodily construction is not incidental to larger social arrangements. As Elizabeth Grosz (1994, 60) has argued, "patriarchy is psychically produced [through] the constitution of women's bodies as lacking." Convincing both men and women that women's bodies are lacking is a cultural project; while boys may understandably see women's bodies as missing what they possess, girls require a more extensive shift. Further linking bodily difference to qualities of mind is essential to representing men as powerful and privileged; in Grosz's phrasing, "if women do not lack in any ontological sense (there is no lack in the real, as Lacan is fond of saying), men cannot be said to have" (ibid.). Masculinity can be phallic only because femininity is vulnerable, castrated, unfixed.

This oppositional dependence means that the phallic position is continually a position full of anxiety. The project of being a phallic subject always contains the threat of being overcome by that which it excludes; the phallic subject always runs the risk of being exposed as needy and incomplete. In Susan Bordo's observation, "actual men are not timeless symbolic constructs; they are biologically, historically, and experientially embodied beings; the singular, constant, transcendent rule of the phallus is continually challenged by this embodiment" (1997, 31–32). Thus the phallic, self-contained subject inevitably generates its own outside, an outside that threatens to unmask actual men as impostors. The vulnerability of actual bodies, both male and female, threatens men with the removal of authority.

Many, if not most, bodies cannot aspire to full phallic status. Some suffer from femininity, others from a hypermasculinity that is inconsistent with liberal citizenship. Feminine bodies, whether female or male, are those that "leak" across the boundaries of the phallic imagination.

Such bodies may literally leak, as in menstruation, or they may allow for receptivity and thus be "passive," vulnerable to others. In either case, they are understood to present incomplete boundaries and thus represent the possibility of threats to the masculine self. In Grosz's words, "in the West, in our time, the female body has been constructed not only as a lack or absence but with more complexity, as a leaking, uncontrollable, seeping liquid; as formless flow; as viscosity, entrapping, secreting; as lacking not so much or simply the phallus but self-containment—not a cracked or porous vessel, like a leaking ship, but a formlessness that engulfs all form, a disorder than threatens all order" (1994, 203). Such a being must be subordinated in order for the phallic self to avoid being overcome.

The hypermasculine body, such as the body of the slave or his sons, is too much body rather than a leaky one. It threatens the masculine body even as it seems to exemplify it. The hypermasculine body is the result of too much corporeality and not enough time in an armchair. The exposure of the hypermasculine body leads to its emasculation, rather than its feminization. In other words, it loses its authority as a consequence of "too much" embodiment. Although black athletes in the United States are exemplars of one form of masculinity, it is not a form that carries cultural authority or increases the power of black people in general (Connell 1995). In fact, as Bordo (1997, 37) notes, racist discourses that force Black men "to carry the shadow of instinct, of unconscious urge, of the body itself—and hence of the penis-as-animal, powerful and exciting by virtue of brute strength and size, but devoid of phallic will and conscious control" serve not to enhance respect and authority but to undermine it. Similarly, the hypermasculinity of some gay men serves to open them to violence and hatred rather than inclusion. Phallic masculinity is characterized by initiative and activity, but also by self-control. Exposure of too much of the male body, or of finely honed male bodies, may draw some admiring looks but works to disqualify one from liberal citizenship. The fiction that the male body is not really a body is belied not only by men who craft their bodies, but also by men who use them "too much," whether in work, in swagger, or in violence. It is also, as Lee Quinby (1999, 1084) notes, present in biotechnologies that manifest "the millenialist desire for bodily perfection," a perfection she identifies as persistently masculinist.

This "imaginary anatomy," in Jacques Lacan's phrasing, has profound implications for politics. The quintessential capacities of the modern citizen, autonomy and self-control, are associated with the limited embodiment of the masculine self. These capacities are then conferred upon those whose actual anatomy is seen to accord with it. The liberal citizen is normatively not only male, but masculine, white, and heterosexual. Not only is the citizen delineated by race, gender, and sexuality; the body politic as a whole shares the attributes of the citizen. The imaginary anatomy of the body politic is masculine, and it serves to exclude, in Moira Gatens's phrase, "those whose corporeal specificity marks them as inappropriate analogues to the body politic" (1991, 82). The exclusion of "others" is not a function of their corporeality alone, but of the wrong corporeality—a corporeality that on the one hand opens them to others and potentially subjects them to another's will, but on the other hand offers a mode of embodiment that threatens the phallic citizen.

Political Passions

Although liberal theories have trouble with embodiment, they do by and large recognize passion. In liberal theory, however, passions seem to be features of minds that have no clear connection to bodies. Bodies appear in liberal theory as vulnerable—to pain, to hunger and cold, to attack. The asceticism of this view of the body is indebted to a Stoic-inflected Christianity. Liberal theory evokes threats to the body, challenging phallic masculinity, in order to suggest schemes of rescue. The ideal of ordered liberty requires bodily comfort, but liberals disagree on whether this is the ultimate goal of politics. For Locke and Hobbes, physical security seems to be the main virtue of civil society. For Rousseau and Kant, however, the goal of government is the establishment of autonomy among citizens. All of these theorists agree that passions tell us about our particular desires, but that they are not to be followed. Rather, Hobbes and Locke hope to substitute interest for passion, precisely because it is more stable and permanent. Reason follows interest and constrains passion.

Among the passions to be disciplined is love. Love is not to be eliminated, but it is to be relegated to "private" life, specifically the family.

Love binds, but it also inspires conflict; in either case it is too particu-
laristic for politics. Liberal theorists have no room for love, just as they
have none for hatred or any other disruptive passion. The goal of liberal politics is not to build relations of sympathy or solidarity, nor to rely
on them, but rather to make the world safe for masculine bodies.

Speaking of the tradition of contract theory, Carole Pateman (1989,
4) has noted that the classic texts tell us that women "cannot transcend
their bodily natures and sexual passions": "Women's bodies symbolize
everything opposed to political order." For the contract tradition, with
its concern to replace or moderate passion with reason, women's exclusion has been justified by their inability to control themselves.

Although Pateman's analysis of the exclusion of emotion and bodies
applies to liberal theory, however, it is less satisfactory for understanding republicanism. Both the liberal and the republican bodies are phallic in their impermeability and autonomy, but they have quite different
relations to citizen bodies and to the passions. Discerning this difference
offers us a more nuanced portrait of contemporary American citizenship
than that afforded by critics of liberalism alone. The originary and continuing role of republicanism in American political thought mandates
consideration of republicanism both in its classical varieties and in
American political life.

Passions are important for liberals but are to be removed from the
public sphere as much as possible. For civic republicans, on the other
hand, love and hate are the foundations of polities. As Hannah Pitkin
(1984, 26) describes Machiavelli's view, "the city is a woman and the
citizens are her lovers"; or, in the words of Pericles, citizens should
"gaze, day after day, upon the power of the city, and become her
lovers" (Thucydides II.43.1). This view appears in a number of per-
mutations, most prominently in times of war. Whether motherland,
fatherland, or simply Uncle Sam, the polity figured in republican rhetoric is an object of adoration and devotion and the citizens are children
who must fight to protect the threatened parent.

The most important republican passion is love—for one's country,
for its laws, and for one's fellow citizens. This love is an important contrast to the liberal who is either passionless (in the Kantian and Rawl-
sian models) or whose passion is in need of subduing (Hobbes, Locke).
Summarizing Machiavelli's view, Pitkin notes that "without passion

and struggle, there can be no liberty, but only reification, habit, and drift" (300). This passion is a love for one's country and for one's countrymen, the fellow sons of the city.

Republican love, however, is narrowly bounded. It is a love simultaneously personal and abstract, in which others are loved as citizens but not as individuals. Citizens are not loved by other citizens because of their personal virtues or qualities, but because they are fellow citizens. The primary love is for one's country; love of one's fellow citizens flows, as it were, in a circuit from citizen to country to citizen, much as Christians are held to love one another through their love of Christ. The republican's love is intense, allowing for self-sacrifice even to death, but it is not a love of persons but of the idea of persons, or of the country as a person.[1]

This intense yet abstract love is curiously similar to certain formations of phallic masculinity. What earlier feminist theorists labeled "abstract masculinity," in which masculinity derives its content solely from its contrast to femininity (cf. Hartsock 1983), has a political corollary in republican citizenship. Republican citizens do not love their country completely abstractly; most writers agree on the importance of particular geography and national features to the love of one's country. But the love of one's fellow citizens, which must be abstract given that one cannot know them all, much less love them all, is rather a love for the idea of one's fellow citizens. It is not a particular love, but a universal love—a curious blend.

One of the primary threats to such citizenly love is the particular love for another, especially romantic love. From Aristotle to Machiavelli to Rousseau, and latent in today's controversies over queer citizenship, we find the concern that romantic love's "particularizing" force has the potential to destroy polities. There are several reasons for this power. First, romantic love makes for preferences among citizens. Such preferences may lead one to neglect one's civic duty in order to protect or privilege loved ones. Second, romantic love creates conflicts between men and within each man as he wrestles between civic and romantic love (Aristotle 1911, 1311a–b). Romantic love has the potential for neglect of duty and for internal division as men love women over their country.

Most republican theorists and politicians have resolved this problem by privatizing women so that each man emerges in the public world as

"citizen x" rather than "Joe who got my girl." They seek not to eliminate romantic love, but to wall it off. Controlling women is a crucial element of what Pateman has described as "fraternal patriarchy" (1988).
Such control is not unique to republicanism; indeed, Pateman's focus is
on liberal theory. As she notes, however, the liberal citizen is defined "in
opposition to the political and the masculine passions" that are central
to republican understandings. The republican fraternal contract does
not require the elimination of such passions, but constrains their disruptive effects by controlling women. Thus, the good republican society
requires sharp sexual differentiation and separation in order to allow for
the mutual dependence of free men (Rousseau 1913; Schwartz 1984).

Homosocial passions are not only safe in such a society, they are
required as an element of fraternity. Their free flow depends upon a
pattern of simultaneous acknowledgment and denial: acknowledgment
of their fraternal love and commitment with denial of any sexual or
erotic elements.

A recognition, even an embrace, of passion should not be mistaken
for an idealization of a less phallic body. The passionate citizen is inner-
directed, with passions moving outward toward others but never being
penetrated by fashion or the whims of others. The focus on discipline
is not a denial of passion, but urges its channeling from formlessness to
phallic ordering. Through their love of the city, citizens conceive themselves as simultaneously passionate and controlled. One does not
demonstrate manly virtue by lack of passion but through conquering it,
manifesting one's strength (Monoson 1994).

In David Halperin's treatment of the Athenian citizen body, he
argues that democracy produced "a new kind of body—a free, autonomous, and inviolable body undifferentiated by distinctions of wealth,
class, or status: a democratic body, the site and guarantee of personal and
political independence" (1990, 98). Political equality was premised on
the self-understandings of male citizens as "lords over their own bodies" (99), in contrast to all those who lacked such authority—women,
slaves, children, foreigners. Although "homosexuality" was acceptable,
adult male citizens were enjoined to participate only as penetrators.
Allowing oneself to be penetrated, then as now, was evidence of one's
unfitness for equality. It must be noted that the failure was not of excessive passion, for the *eromenos* was not seen as passionate, but rather of a

willingness to be receptive. The passionate citizen was crucial to the welfare of the polity, but the passions had to be "manly" ones.

Both Monoson and Pitkin note the importance of mutuality in this understanding. Because citizens cannot be subordinate or submissive to others, both the Periclean and the Machiavellian versions of republicanism work to provide a vision of connection that does not violate the phallic conception of the citizen. Thus both suggest that politics is not a matter of domination of fellow citizens, but is a relationship among manly peers; those who can be dominated do not belong. This vision of mutuality, however, is constantly interrupted. Eros is continually figured for Machiavelli in terms of domination and possession (Pitkin 1984, 25, 301). The full mutuality of citizens evoked in republican literature is interwoven with images of threat and contest. Love of the polity does not mean submission to it, or even respectful consideration of the many persons in it, but instead legitimates domination in the name of the savior. As lovers of the city, citizens may decide what the beloved shall do and be.

War is a prominent, but not the only, scene that calls forth such passionate images. In general, for republicans passion and struggle are the means to ensure freedom. Complacency is the greatest danger to republics. From Pericles to Theodore Roosevelt, republican politicians have excoriated complacency and narrow self-interest. The author of the Cato letters in eighteenth-century America wrote that "virtue is the passion for pursuing the public good, with which the lesser passions may compete, but into which they may equally be transformed" (quoted in Pocock 1975, 472). The public realm is, in his understanding, "a device or mechanism for requiring men . . . to erect an edifice of reason and virtue on a foundation of passion" (ibid.). A century later, Roosevelt stressed that the character of a citizen must combine "resolution, courage, energy, power of self-control, combined with fearlessness in taking the initiative and assuming responsibility" (3). Indeed, for Roosevelt "the democratic ideal must be that of subordinating chaos to order" (12). The goal of education for citizenship is to produce men who can see the good, desire it, and will its enactment. His stress on discipline and obedience to the law recalls Abraham Lincoln's exhortations to obey the law, exhortations rooted in a keen appreciation for the vitality and the volatility of passion (1992, 16–19).

This ideal is deeply imbricated with cultural conceptions of gender. The American Revolutionary generation explicitly maintained the republican dichotomies of independence/dependence, constancy/fickleness, control/license as measures not only of women's distance from men, but also of the failings of individual men. This was not incidental to their project, as Linda Kerber (1997) notes: among that generation, as for earlier and later republicans, "anxieties for the stability of their construction led them, as they emphasized its reasonableness, its solidity, its link to classical models, also to emphasize its manliness and its freedom from effeminacy. The construction of the autonomous, patriotic male citizen required that the traditional identification of women with unreliability, unpredictability, and lust be emphasized" (264).

Kerber points out that these associations run throughout the twentieth century as well, as manifested in university curricula in "American civilization" (221). The distinction between manly and "weak" passions continues today, sometimes under the code of "will" versus "emotion." Those who display vulnerability directly, through tears or the expression of compassion, are "emotional"; those otherwise rational men who exhibit anger or frustration are "strong" or "forceful." Sometimes those who manifest anger or frustration are not authorized to do so, by virtue of their embodied status; when they do so, they are emotional rather than forceful. We cannot say simply that some passions are manly and others are not. We must look at who is displaying them, how, and for what cause. When Secretary of State Madeleine Albright shows anger with Saddam Hussein she is strong; were she to display such vehemence concerning women's oppression or on behalf of queer equality, I suspect she would be seen as hysterical.

Women can nonetheless have civic passion in republican theory. Although they are not to be direct combatants, women's role as mothers and their extension of that role to support of the body politic requires passionate love of their country. It is not the amount of passion that disqualifies women from full citizenship, but the nature of their passion—fickle, inconstant—and their inability to control themselves. The body politic requires the support of those who can be counted upon to defend it with their lives.

Laboring Citizens

American citizenship is no longer understood simply as a matter of bearing arms, voting, and being concerned with public honor. The social standing central to citizenship is found before the law and in politics, to be sure, but more importantly it is to be found in "the marketplace, in production and commerce, in the world of work in all its forms, and in voluntary associations" (Shklar 1991, 63). Here is where a citizen finds "his social place, his standing, the approbation of his fellows, and possibly some of his self-respect" (ibid.). Pateman (1989, 184) agrees with this assessment of paid employment and links both citizenship and work to the notions of ownership and contribution. Workers contribute to their society, thus earning citizenship as well as a wage. Modern welfare states have not treated domestic labor as "work" relevant to citizenship, overlooking the contribution of many women. Further, since domestic labor does not lead to ownership or even a wage, those whose work is in the home or who cannot work are not recognized as having a stake in public affairs (10). In such a regime, not working amounts to the loss of public presence as well as approval. Those who do not work cannot be independent; and if they are not independent they are not only less than equal, they are a drain on those who work. In contemporary American society, the threat of luxury and corruption so central to republican rhetoric bears the faces of welfare mothers, slackers, and immigrants, as well as sexual minorities.

The fetishization of labor has perpetuated the myth of phallic agency. The laboring body endures; it is disciplined; it is productive. In the United States, the laboring body is the citizen body. Bodies that fail identification with the laboring body must be suspect as citizen bodies. Not all citizen bodies labor, of course, but the citizen ideal in the United States labors in the market. The individual who is cared for by others—whether by family members or the state—is not considered a worker, and thus does not present herself as a citizen (Fraser and Gordon 1994a, 1998; Pateman 1989, 179–209; Young 1997, ch. 6). Her body is not seen as a laboring body, because its labor is invisible to the market. Women's campaigns for access to work relied on this point, treating work as the precondition of effective citizenship. This ideal of labor has limited the progress of social rights in the United States. Not only are women who don't earn treated as less than equal, their homes and bodies open for state inspection, men who fail to produce are often denied even the minimal welfare allotted to women and children. The ideology of phallic masculinity mandates that any man worth his citizenship be a worker. The absence of welfare, training programs, and other social support for single men signals a widespread willingness to deny acknowledgment to those who don't act like "real men."

The peculiar importance of work, Shklar argues, arises from the centrality of the contrast between free and slave in U.S. history. She describes the "American work ethic" as "the ideology of citizens caught between racist slavery and aristocratic pretensions," an ideology that has endured because the political conditions to which it responded from the first have not disappeared" (1991, 64). The phallic binary of agent/slave may have its roots in this unique situation. The stark division between free and slave has always been a resonant and overused part of American political language. Slavery is not a sufficient explanation, however; republican language employed such binaries well before it crossed the Atlantic. Slavery gave a particular vividness to the division, a visible threat to match the rhetoric, but republicanism has always relied on the distinction between free and slave to make its point about the need for the equal status and participation of citizens.

The ideology of labor should not obscure the fact that late capitalism thrives on producing consumers rather than workers. The actual situation of the contemporary United States is much more complex than the ideology of labor suggests. "In our time," Zygmunt Bauman writes, "individuals are engaged (morally by society, functionally by the social system) first and foremost as consumers rather than producers" (1988, 807; see also Cooper 1993; Evans 1993). Neo-liberal discourse has made a virtue of this shift, addressing citizens as consumers of social goods. Not only has citizenship become a matter of consuming governmental services, however; it has become just as much an issue of patterns of private consumption (buying U.S.A., using boycotts to express disapproval of corporate policies, etc.). Nonetheless, the ideology maintains labor as a crucial part of American identity and a central rhetorical figure in public policy debates (see, e.g., Galston 1991). Only certain potential "customers" "deserve" to consume public goods, as the rampant efforts to penalize nonofficial immigrants make clear. Those who do not labor (or those who labor without authorization) are ineligible for the consumption of citizenship.

The association of citizenship and labor suggests a fruitful avenue for understanding the position of LBGT people. The sexual body invoked by gay, lesbian, and queer political campaigns directly challenges the working body of the laboring citizen. Citizenship and labor both require discipline and renunciation. Although campaigns for equality do not emphasize sexual practice, the very identity that is stigmatized invokes sexual desire and the promise of pleasure; furthermore, the heavy focus within these debates on gay men and the fact that men are the primary policy and opinion makers means that those most directly governed by the ideology of phallic masculinity are being haunted by their other. Pleasure, present in republican thought only as luxury and corruption, is trying to work its way into citizen bodies. Thus campaigns for sexual equality run directly counter to both liberal disembodiment and republican phallicism.

Which sexual renunciations are called for in order to become citizens? More directly, what is the status of work that mixes labor and sex? The contradictions faced by sex workers, legal and illegal, are profound. Free labor has been one of the great integrating forces in the United States, as immigrants earned respect through work. Civil rights, beginning with the right to settle in the United States, have often hinged on one's status as an employable worker. On the other hand, the manifestation of sexuality (other than working-class white masculinity) has been considered a disqualification for full membership. Those who cannot or will not isolate their sexual bodies from their working bodies pose a major challenge to the theory and practice of citizenship. Sexual minorities have not been allowed to desexualize their working bodies. This denial, and its accompanying denial of equality, has shaped the terms of assimilation for sexual strangers. We will see in subsequent chapters that the imperative of desexualization is both understandable and doomed to failure.

Phallic Agency and Civil Rights

Under the pressure of feminist movements, the earlier explicit exclusion of women from political membership has been attenuated. Women in the United States today are accorded many (though not all) of the rights conferred upon men, and are widely viewed as citizens. This has not, however, spelled the end of phallic masculinity. Instead, the phallic mode has broadened in modernity, especially the United States, into a formation I will refer to as phallic agency. The phallic agent, whether male, female, or something else, is imagined to possess the invulnerability and activity characteristic of phallic masculinity. In the discourse of phallic agency, agency is equated with initiative as opposed to receptivity or transmission, and with invulnerability as opposed to "being a victim." Agency becomes an either/or proposition: either I am fully self-initiating, acting from my own deepest motives and beliefs (that of course are uniquely mine and not the result of socialization or other inscriptions), letting nothing stand between me and my dreams; or I am a victim, a weakling, a dupe, a slave. To the phallic agent, there are actors and there are the acted-upon. Although traditionally this division was held to map neatly onto men and women, white and non-white, the discourse of equality over the past three centuries has fostered lines of migration across these categories. Without changing the binary, those previously held to be passive have found ways to imagine themselves as phallic and have made claims to equality based on their shared phallic status.

Of course this is not all that has happened; social movements have also challenged the binary between phallic agents and victims, often quite powerfully. Movements of oppressed peoples always embody the tension between claiming political attention on the basis of what has been done to one and acting on one's own behalf; such movements are movements of victim/agents. Nonetheless, in American culture these binaries remain defaults for understanding social status, and the position of the victim/agent is continually refused and vilified. The stereotype of "victim feminism," propounded by popular authors, male and female alike, concedes that women may and should be able to be independent, equal citizens while excoriating virtually all feminist analyses for their "obsession" with barriers to equality and independence (Deutchman 1998). The phallic response is to deny that women or other groups are systematically disempowered, and to view as insulting the claim that they are.

Investment in the phallic imaginary anatomy enables us to understand not only the overt rejection of those whose bodies do not conform to that imaginary anatomy, but also the stigmatization of civil rights claims when made by such non-conforming embodied subjects. There are at least two discourses on civil rights in the United States, and their contradictory reception and employment are understandable through the lens of the phallic body politic. These discourses are linked to differing understandings about what is being claimed and who is claiming it.

The first discourse, familiar since before the American Revolution, demands certain basic rights for citizens, understood to be male heads of households. These rights include safety within and control over one's household; protection from violence, both by individuals and the state; and the right to participate in public decision-making through freedom of speech and association. Insisting upon these rights is part of being a man in the United States; failure to do so would be "wimpy," ignoble, a demonstration of weakness. Masculinity in the United States is closely bound up with the maintenance of one's rights.

When others use this discourse, however, their discordant personal features threaten the body politic. What in the hands of white heterosexual men serves as the foundation of liberty becomes an attack on society when extended to those who were previously either incorporated into the polity through the "head" of the household or excluded from recognition. The Revolutionary generation and those to follow confronted the dilemma of how to claim the language of equality and natural law for themselves while denying it to others; this task was usually managed, to the extent that it was managed, first by claiming irrevocable differences between the characters and capacities of male citizens and those they sought to exclude, and second by the division between public and private realms. Public equality of men relied upon their mutual privilege and domination of women, children, and people of color (Kerber 1997; Pateman 1998). With the rise of feminism and consequent refigurings of law, the demand for safety within one's household becomes a ban on marital assault, rape, and incest. The recognition that many citizens live within a household, and that they may not in fact share the interest of the eldest male, allows the state to penetrate the household in new ways, piercing the castle walls and besieging that "miniature fatherland" through which Rousseau (1911, 326) believed that attachment to the larger fatherland, the state, was accomplished. In Rousseau's time as in ours, "the desire to retain in the traditional form of marriage some safeguard of order against the destructive tendencies of modern individualism, cut across the familiar divides between conservative and liberal, left and right" (Vogel 1994, 76). It also cuts across lines of gender and race. Civil liberties meant to foster the independence of male citizens against the state become instruments of destruction when wielded by those who cannot legitimately claim to be "heads."

The shift in the nature of rights depending upon who has them is only part of the story, however. Just as important is the change in understandings of what rights are needed for basic citizenship. The second discourse of rights addresses what T. H. Marshall (1992) calls "social rights"—rights to education, decent housing, and food. These rights have never been completely accepted in the United States. Although they are widely acknowledged as prerequisites for the independence associated with citizenship, the individualism of the United States has blocked their full incorporation into rights. This failure is not simply due to an abstraction that we may call individualism, however. Rather, the particular form of American individualism is crucial for understanding the resistance to these social rights. American individualism, like its republican counterpart, is deeply gendered. In fact, it is not too much to say that "the classic statements of American individualism are best understood as guides to masculine identity" (Kerber 1997, 202). From Emerson to Horatio Alger to contemporary fiction and political writing, the heroic individual is male and masculine. He works hard, he thinks for himself, and he stands firm for his principles and his family in the face of danger and seduction.

The political experience of groups figured as non-phallic makes clear that civil rights are not a single package with a consistent response, either within individuals or within communities. The demand for civil rights puts one in the position of admitting one's vulnerability and dependence on the larger society. Such admissions are often viewed as whining excuses by those who want to imagine themselves as intact and their society as composed of similarly bounded individuals. Phallic agents of whatever group see the admission of inequality as the abandonment of agency, and so are just as prone to attack those speaking in their behalf as they are to question those who would exclude them. The American citizen is figured in popular imagination as an effective agent, capable of making real change. That figure both endorses and works against movements for equality. On the one hand, for the citizen to make change she must see problems and convince others of their gravity and the possibility of change. On the other hand, admitting some problems threatens the citizen's certainty that she is in fact a citizen, opening the door to feelings of rejection and abandonment that she may not be willing to confront. In order to become an oppositional agent, one must first admit one's discontent and present ineffectiveness; in a culture in which feelings of inefficacy are held to be pathological, individuals are reluctant to follow that path. This continuing dynamic of social movements must be confronted, and not simply diagnosed as false consciousness; without finding ways of penetrating phallic masculinity, movements for change will continually face the charge that they, rather than the circumstances they oppose, stand in the way of equality.

Drives for citizenship continually fail to challenge the inequalities, injuries, and injustices committed by the polity, other than that of excluding a particular group. The fiction presented in such drives is that of a homogeneous citizenry, contented with their government and society. The demand for inclusion reinforces this fiction, and thus reinforces the phallic citizen. On the other hand, however, such drives run the risk of building a case for inclusion simply on the basis of injury. Here the focus of argument is the wrong done to the group by exclusion. The group is then forced to account for itself as incomplete, dependent subjects who could be phallic citizens with a bit of help. This paradox prevents the demand for citizenship from going beyond inclusion to a broader vision of social transformation and justice, and so maintains the structures of citizenship that produced the exclusion.

Wendy Brown (1995) has described the limitations of an identity built on injury. In her analysis identity politics is rooted in the interplay between subjectivities formed through disciplinary apparatuses and the liberal demand for inclusion in an imaginary space of equality. The effect of this confluence is twofold. On the one hand, the liberal element has continually pushed identity politics away from larger critiques of existing societies, especially structures of exploitation endemic to capitalism. The idealized surface of a society whose only failure is the exclusion of certain categories of people leads to a reduction of social criticism in favor of simple demands for "equality." This element is most visible in contemporary demands for same-sex marriage and military service. Rather than using exclusion as a vantage point from which to criticize these central institutions of patriarchal nation-states, advocates are claiming these institutions as marks of personal dignity and social worth.

On the other hand, contemporary forms of identity politics, gay and lesbian activism included, derive much of their energy from the sense of injury that is central to identity formation of their subjects. In saying this, I want to make clear that the sense of injury is not caused by identity politics (or not only by it). Systems of stigmatization and subordination do indeed injure the subjects produced through their operations. The injury is constitutive of the identity. Because of this, the identity feeds on *ressentiment*, on the re-experiencing of injury. Identity politics is a response to, a demand for the end of, such injury. Nonetheless, as Brown points out, "identity structured by *ressentiment* at the same time becomes invested in its own subjection" (1995, 216). As identity politics uses *ressentiment* to motivate subordinated groups, it does not challenge injury so much as reinscribe it. Without a vision of a desired future, such a politics amounts to a continual picking at the scab of suffering. In this instance, "[p]oliticized identity, premised on exclusion and fueled by the humiliation and suffering imposed by its historically structured impotence in the context of a discourse of sovereign individuals, is as likely to seek generalized political paralysis, to feast on generalized political impotence, as it is to seek its own or collective liberation through empowerment" (217).

Nor are "minorities" the only perpetrator/victims of this disciplinary nexus. William Connolly (1995) has made clear the links between modern masculinity, injury, and revenge. In explaining the resurgence of a variety of fundamentalisms in America, Connolly describes the process by which working-class youths come to see themselves as victims: in their own eyes, "this constituency is first inducted into a masculine ideal, then feminized through the structure and insecurity of the work available to it, then assaulted in its masculinity by representatives of the gender it is supposed to govern and protect, and finally courted by right-wing elites who idealize the very model of masculine assertion that has been promised and denied" (114).

The phallic citizen is continually under attack, both from within through the impossibility of completion and from without by the gap between the ideal of invulnerability and mastery and the reality of economic and political subordination. As a result, a new identity politics has taken shape around "the endangered American male."[2] Such endangered men are caught between the American liberal commitment to equality and the residuum of privilege and subordination that continues to define male masculinity. Thus, the second element of the interaction between disciplinary structures and liberal politics feeds off of the failure of the first. Liberalism's inability to project a vision of the common good combines with identities formed through disciplinary forms of exclusion and subordination to produce a politics whose only goal is normalization under the sign of equality. Convinced that exclusion is injury and injury always exclusion, this version of identity politics becomes on the one hand an interest-group politics, and on the other a permanent grievance. As we will see in Chapter 4, much current gay political writing is informed by this grievance and the goal of normalization. To such a view, citizenship might appear to be the ultimate good. Contemporary citizenship offers (at least the promise of) equal recognition and dignity; it seems to offer the end of injury and the fulfillment of phallic agency, as queers and other others are acknowledged by the majority as worthwhile members of the polity. As we have seen, however, that agency is itself fraught with injury and ressentiment; citizenship will not spell the end of these but their generalization.

The Body under Siege

Republican political theorists such as Machiavelli and Rousseau have agreed that liberty is the fruit of struggle, and that its maintenance requires constant vigilance and valor. But if struggle must be continual, against whom is it to be directed? One of the greatest dangers of civic republicanism is its need for an enemy, whether internal or external, in order to marshal the citizen body. This marshaling is simultaneously a constitution, both of the enemy and of the citizen self. The perception of threat is not incidental or subsequent to the construction of the republican citizen self, but is integral to that constitution. The citizen must constantly ward off threats to the autonomy and sovereignty of the body, both the personal body and the body politic, in order to establish his own autonomy and sovereignty. Citizenship is about virility, active defense of that which is threatened rather than being the victim of threat. At moments of threat, republican rhetoric denies the threat to masculine individuals and instead figures the country as threatened in need of the defense of her sons and the obedience of her daughters. Thus anxiety about personal security is disavowed and displaced onto another vulnerable body.

The trope of the body politic works powerfully to transform contests within society into attacks on society. Stigmatized groups may become threats to "the public health" and the "moral fiber of the nation," imagined agents of disintegration. These threats are threats to the phallic status of the public body: the body politic is threatened by "becoming soft," by being "susceptible," "docile," "passive," "infected"—in short, by being either penetrated or vulnerable to penetration (Mosse 1985; Stychin 1998, 9).

In the United States, sexuality has been a primary site for fears of contamination of the body politic. It is possible to understand this in liberal terms, as simply the result of ignorance or outmoded religious strictures, and that is not a false understanding. It is, however, incomplete. These fears are integral to the phallic self, and mitigating them requires a transformation of that self. The challenge of queers is not simply about sexual difference, but about the very passions that constitute American understandings of citizenship.

The Revolutionary period demonstrates the links between individual imagery and political imaginaries. In tracing the gendered fears and hopes of the Revolutionary generation, Kerber notes that "the men who remodeled the American polity after the war remodeled it in their own image. Their anxieties for the stability of their construction led them, as they emphasized its reasonableness, its solidity, its link to classical models, also to emphasize its manliness and its freedom from effeminacy" (1997, 264). This construction and its attendant anxieties has continued throughout American history, visible not only in the republican pronouncements of Abraham Lincoln and Theodore Roosevelt but also in every military action or social crisis (Weber 1999). The threat is both internal and external: invasion from without, and corruption within, are equally powerful and devastating attacks on the phallic body politic.

The threat to the phallic body of the citizen posed by homosexuality is by now clear to many. The fears about gays in the military, fears that cluster around the shower and the barracks, are so clear as to need no analysis. Heterosexual soldiers' repeated expressions of concern that someone might be looking at them or wanting to touch them, expressions solicited and encouraged by their military superiors and by senators, make manifest a host of assumptions about masculine sexuality and the privilege of looking. For these men, being a man means being the initiator, the gazer, the penetrator, but never the one penetrated by gaze or by body, never the object of another's initiative. Homosexuality here becomes problematic because while homosexuality is the most explicit celebration of male bodies and masculinity, it also is a threat to the system of sexual difference within which masculinity takes on meaning. Fear of violation and its activating assumptions is present not only in discussions of the military, but in virtually every treatment of queers in politics. Whether the individual body or the national body, some body is being threatened by strange desire.

The entry of acknowledged homosexuality into this scene is a threat for several reasons. First, acknowledgment of some men's erotic love threatens the structure of denial on which fraternity depends. Following Freud, Judith Butler (1997, 120) argues that "social feeling and citizenship" are founded on a desexualized and externalized homosexuality. Desire shapes social bonds as well as resentments. In this argument, the acknowledgment of civic or fraternal love is fraught with disruptive potential and seems to mandate the withdrawal of civic passion altogether. By making homosociality no longer innocent, gay men threaten not only the phallic masculine self but the possibilities for love among heterosexual men. This is of course a great loss to republican men, one they might understandable resent. The homosexual man becomes the spoiler, the wet blanket at the fraternal slumber party.

Acknowledging queer love would also endanger the polity through the reintroduction of particular love. If love between men is possible, it threatens the polity just as romantic love for women did. Love between men, however, can't be dealt with by isolating the potential object of affection and contest; since such love may ignite from any man who opens himself to it, the opening itself must be squashed. This can be ensured (never successfully) only by enforcing heterosexual marriage as an imperative and removing those who manifest the possibility of opening to other men.

If the military must be protected as a zone for male homosociality, families must be both defended and used as weapons against sexual chaos. The assumption of naturalness surrounding the heterosexual nuclear family would seem to ensure that it will weather social change, but its bodyguards have made clear that, as David Schneider (1968) found, this is a natural phenomenon that needs social engineering to succeed. Nuclear families provide the only template for sexual order in our society. As we will see, efforts by sexual minorities to overcome their position as strangers repeatedly invoke sexual order and naturalness. Whether this is a subversive remaking or an assimilationism that cannot work will be discussed in chapter 4.

Citizenship for those whose bodies and passions do not conform to phallic modes will require not simply citizenship for queers, but a thorough queering of citizenship itself. Such a queering must include a challenge to the ideology of independence and masculinity. As the grounds for citizenship, the ideology of independence and its not-so-covert gendered association continue to make strangers out of women, queers, and others who do not fit the ideal of the autonomous individual. "The community" remains the community of male heads of households, with their families in a zone somewhere between public and private. Activism that challenges associations between heterosexuality, whiteness, and masculinity with autonomous rationality will inevitably confront the rhetoric of the citizen body and the body politic, and my earlier remarks should not be construed as suggesting that reaction is a reason not to engage in such challenges. We must, however, seek to fully understand the contours and the functioning of such rhetoric. We cannot simply use liberal arguments and trust in the triumph of reason, both because history shows us that reason does not always triumph and because reason itself is bound up in the contention. Disentangling the elements of citizenship rhetoric may enable us to perform micro-challenges, placing pressure on weak points and easing republican discourse into forms that are less rigid and oppositional. This, at any rate, is my hope.

3

Structures of Strangeness
Citizenship and Kinship

At the end of the nineteenth century, Congress was faced with a series of decisions about polygamy. The practice of polygamy among Mormons, most notably in Utah but also in Idaho, was the subject of popular outcry as these territories moved toward statehood. Groups opposed to statehood demanded laws banning polygamy throughout the United States, and prospective voters in Utah were forced to sign an oath foreswearing "polygamy, bigamy, unlawful cohabitation, incest, adultery, and fornication" (U.S. Congress 1890, 1). Such oaths did not settle the issue; legislators and citizens continued to hunt down polygamists and ban them from citizenship rights. Mormons were characterized as "absolutely treacherous," suffering from moral decay that produced children who were "a menace to the future of our country" (U.S. Congress 1902, 2) because of the "licentiousness" to which they were exposed. The full rhetoric of the body under siege was mobilized against the heathens, who had "no right to be called American citizens" (13). Polygamy was a "disease" being "scattered" around the country and, just as "evil is catching in a way that goodness never is" (8), if not stopped it would soon drive out decent family values. No compromise was acceptable, nothing short of national action would suffice: when the body is under siege, compromise or rapprochement cannot be afforded. What compromise is acceptable between a body and an invading agent?

The Mormons, many of whom now spearhead the drive against same-sex marriage, felt that they valued marriage as much as anyone in the United States. What they saw as true, holy marriage was not seen as an "alternative understanding" or an "expansion" of marriage by their antagonists, but as a dagger pointed at the heart of marriage and family life, and through that to the whole body politic. And that is what opponents of same-sex marriage see today—not an opportunity to domesticate those promiscuous queers, but the introduction of chaos into the core of society. Like the polygamous mother, lesbians and gays are depicted as inducting their children into sin in such a way that their children do not even recognize it as sin. Appeals to maternal love and examples of happy families will continually confront the fear that these parents' love will lead their children to accept that which should not be accepted. Maternal love then becomes not domesticating and instructive, but seductive.

It is not a coincidence that the 1990s have offered not one "marriage question," but two. Along with same-sex marriage, against which states and the national government have inoculated themselves via "defense of marriage" laws defining it in heterosexual terms, heavily Mormon states are also confronting a new visibility and debate about polygamy (*New York Times*, December 11, 1997). Participants in these two developments do not recognize one another; indeed, at first these quests seem polar opposites. On the one hand, polygamy violates current U.S. norms by being too archaic and absolute in its patriarchy. On the other hand, same-sex marriage challenges the persistent patriarchy in heterosexual marriage. One differentiates and subordinates too much, the other not enough. Yet these two are twin products of the changes in family realities and norms over the past thirty years. Both polygamists and same-sex couples engage in wedding ceremonies that are not legally recognized, yet carry weight within their communities. Both are increasingly active and vocal in their demand for, and occasional receipt of, recognition. As a polygamist said, "Our parents had a harder time. . . . No one would hire them. Now, people don't care about your personal life. They don't ask, How do you lock up a guy for having two wives when Wilt Chamberlain talks about sleeping with thousands of women? We feel tolerated now for the first time." Although polygamy remains a felony in Utah, increasingly the issues confronting polygamists have become those of architecture rather than law.

Much the same may be said for same-sex couples. Although their marriages are not legally recognized, and performing marriages for them may carry penalties in some states and some religious denominations, marriage has become an increasingly ubiquitous part of gay and lesbian communities. Existing in a nebulous zone in which we "recognize ourselves" (Lewin 1998) with our families and friends while persisting in legal and bureaucratic solitude, queers join their unlikely (and unwilling) allies in disjoining legal from social recognition. For both groups, such recognition remains uneven and insecure not because it is legally barred, but because it is so conceptually alien to the hegemonic American discourse of family. Legal sanction alone would not suffice to solidify recognition (though it would provide a wedge for the cultural battle to be continued); many strangers enjoy protection under the law without ceasing to be strangers. Because citizenship is a cultural as well as a legal category, and one that is intimately intertwined with kinship, both queers and Mormons (not to mention queer Mormons) may expect to remain strangers for the foreseeable future.

It does not follow from the above that "family" is a non-negotiable term. The existence of same-sex families and polygamous families is evidence to the contrary. The Supreme Court's recent review of visitation rights of grandparents represents the Court's willingness to consider evolving notions of family. The final ruling here is less important than the fact of open discussion and struggle. That everyone currently involved in family politics recognizes this is made evident by the diverse groups filing briefs on both sides. For all of their recent ideological placement as "private," family and kinship structures have always been both constitutive of political ones and actively regulated by political authority. No consideration of the citizenship of lesbians and gays can be adequate without an inquiry into the relation between kinship and citizenship.

Ideologies of Kinship

Male and female bodies (and masculine and feminine ones) have been culturally linked to divisions between public and private life. If the paradigmatic laboring body is male, the image of the domestic laborer is female. This is especially important when we seek to understand the structure of debates over marriage and military: if women have been excluded from the military debate, their role in marriage is more balanced. This is not due to feminist activism, however, but follows from dominant conceptions of women's sphere.

The different bodies of the public and private spheres are enacted in differing temporal logics as well. The association of the family with the body is also an acknowledgment of the facts of birth, death, and intergenerational relations. This, indeed, is precisely what is warded off by those theorists who disdain the private realm. For the Greeks and their admirers, the division between public and private is that between what erodes and renews as bodies erode and renew, and that which may shine into eternity. The public is the arena of great deeds, performed before those who can appreciate them. This appreciation requires cultivation, and so is not accessible to children or those who have not been educated properly. Citizens, those who legitimately enter into public space, are adults. Further, although the ages and experience of adults range widely, political theorists by and large ignore such differences and address the citizens as a unified group.

This tendency to ignore age or generational differences among citizens becomes more pronounced to the extent to which citizenship becomes a purely legal category admitting of no gradations of status. Eighteen-year-old citizens have the same legal standing as fifty-year-old citizens, although their social and political standing may be quite different. When citizenship presumes such universality and abstract adulthood, it is seemingly cut off from kinship formations, in which age and status are relevant.

If patterns and criteria for membership are different for kinship and citizenship, so too are schemes and justifications for authority. Families are the very model of patriarchy, characterized by inequality along several dimensions. In patriarchy fathers rule over mothers, parents over children, seemingly by nature. In modernity these patterns have been put under pressure as women claimed intellectual and moral equality with men, and more recently as children have been seen as the bearers of rights even against their parents. Nonetheless, these changes have not been established beyond legal or social contention; in Utah in 1998, for example, patriarchal polygamy is less controversial than same-sex relationships, and children around the world are still treated largely as the property of their parents.

Of course, it is not only liberals who rely on distinctions between public and private, family and polity. Communitarians of all stripes have argued for the importance of family as a counter to the liberal "procedural republic" (Sandel 1984). John O'Neill (1985), for example, sees "familism" as a bulwark against the bureaucratic "therapeutic" state. The family, O'Neill argues, is an inevitable element of human embodiment, and recognition of this fact leads us from "the twin excesses of neo-individualism and statism" to a political discourse that recognizes the family as "the foundation of all civil and political life" (83). Family here offers a model of connectedness that connects the maintenance of life to the creation of free citizens. And as with many other communitarian thinkers. O'Neill's confidence concerning relations within the family, and his pointed remarks concerning feminism's collusion with the state, lead him away from a critical appraisal of existing families as schools of justice. In contrast to the public world of regulated relations, the family is treated as the zone of self-construction and mutual relations, the haven in the heartless world of modern capitalist societies.

These narratives are not the province only of political theorists. David Schneider's work on American kinship found that American culture defines kinship and family relations as "being nature itself, required by nature, or directly determined by nature" to the extent that "it is quite difficult, often impossible, for Americans to see this as a set of cultural constructs and not the biological facts themselves" (Schneider 1968, 116). Because nature is not simply benevolent, however, Americans rely on law to ensure that the "unnatural" elements of nature do not prevail: "In America, it is the order of law, that is, culture, which resolves the contradictions between man and nature, which are contradictions within nature itself" (109). Kinship is treated as the primary realm of nature, beyond culture's ability to change it; as a matter of "blood," rather than (and often opposed to) reason and consent. This view is held by queers as well as heterosexuals, even as they move to create family forms that challenge the association of kinship and nature (Weston 1991, 34).

Both liberal feminists and those inspired by Marxism have treated the contrast between public and private as constitutive of women's subordination in modern Western societies (Engels 1972 [1884]; Okin 1989; Pateman 1988; Vogel 1991, 1994). Although legal treatments of citizenship describe citizens as free and equal regardless of social status, feminists have made clear the heterosexist assumptions and exclusions that structure citizenship both in theory and in practice. Extending to "deviant subjects" the recognitions afforded to "model citizens" fails to account for the specifics of their lives and may introduce distortions and failures of recognition rather than equal participation.

Susan Okin (1989) has argued that no theory of justice can be complete without consideration of family and conjugal relations, and she finds that existing American families fail to meet even the most minimal liberal standards of justice. Their intimate injustices belie as well the communitarian vision of a haven; as Okin points out, the home becomes a haven for men to the exact extent that women do the physical and emotional labor of the family. Not only are families the first school of citizens, not only does personal economic dependence make political independence difficult; the whole construction of public and private, family and polity, must be treated as a linked system if either "realm" is to be properly understood. This does not mean that they are one system, or that they all serve the same ends without contradiction; it simply means that they are co-constructs. Understanding either part requires locating it vis-à-vis the other. Justice is an important consideration not only within families, but in the relation between families and the state. Families are indeed schools in power, justice, and authority, but they are also highly regulated zones of common life. They are not distinct from the polity, but are co-productive of one another.

Feminist critiques of traditional theory and practice have called for public consideration of the family as part of the project of justice and equality for women, and some have explicitly included lesbigay families in their discussions, but they have rarely taken seriously the challenge that we present to ideas of "the family" as composed of a heterosexual adult couple and their children. Okin points to the greater equality among lesbigay couples as a model for heterosexuals, but she does not move such couples from the margins of her analysis to consider them as family forms in which many women and men live, and which might be judged by her argument; instead that argument remains firmly fixed on "the family" as the site of heterosexuals.

What exactly are the assumptions that link kinship and citizenship and maintain heterosexual privilege? First, and most obviously, citizens have been conceived, whether in republican thought or modern liberalism, as free and equal. This has not meant that no inequality is legitimate, but rather that none should be able to compel the obedience or subjection of another. Theorists have disagreed over whether or to what extent economic equality is required for political equality, but all have agreed that citizens should not be bound by law to subordination to another particular person.

This free and equal status has lived, sometimes comfortably and sometimes not, side by side with families in which men rule women. The delineation of family and citizenship as different and opposed realms has worked until recently to exempt families from examination. The split between public and private has not been as complete in fact as it is in some ideologies. Those who treat the two as distinct and opposed nonetheless recognize the reliance of the polity on households, whether as moral training grounds, zones for physical maintenance and species reproduction, or both; male citizens have thus always been seen as familied beings. Laws that regulate marriage and family life, or public decisions not to regulate past a certain point, have been the product of citizens acting in concert to shape their world. If kinship and family have ever been completely removed from public regulation (and I know of no society for which this is the case), certainly modern Western societies have always treated them as matters for public concern and legislation.

Noting that "the regulation of kinship roles is the way groups maintain the continuity of the group in the face of the natality and mortality of its individuals," Jacqueline Stevens (1997, 73) has described the role that marriage plays in the creation of citizens. First, marriage "names the terms of legitimacy that render some children citizens and others aliens"; secondly, "it announces a form of kinship relations" as the norm; third, it marks certain people as "full citizens" (66). The result is a form of marriage with specific racial implications as well as gender inequality. Concerns for intermarriage most notoriously demonstrate the role of kinship in citizenship; such concerns, and laws resulting from them, have been linked to anxieties over the loss of racial supremacy. "Separate but equal" is the excuse for subjugation in kinship no less than in public accommodations, education, or employment. The rule violated by same-sex marriage is not simply "boy-girl" pairing, but male-female pairing with female subordination. This is of a piece with other legislation and court rulings that maintain the status of the "husband-father" as the privileged element in the family (70–76).

In spite of the recognition of the privileged place of the husband-father, it would be a mistake to think of the relation between kinship and citizenship as simply one of status versus contract. Some might say that citizenship is the product of contract and choice, part of the "public" realm, while kinship is a status relationship into which one is thrown (or, in the case of marriage, a legal status one adopts in accordance with nature). But this opposition is not as neat or as viable as it sounds. Citizens are not generally created through affirmation or contract, but more commonly are born into a status relationship—that of citizenship—with their arrival in a family. This status is widely viewed as "natural," part of one's birthright. Even those who change citizenship (who are "naturalized") usually enter the new country through family relations. Thus, the lines between potential citizens and those who lack the potential (or must prove unusual merit and worth to the host country) are drawn by kinship.

In contrast, marriage and family relations are widely understood, both culturally and legally, as matters of status, with fixed rules of obligation and relation. Precisely this view prevented women from gaining equality in marriage, as their status as wives was held to bind them in subjection to their husbands. It is clear, however, that marriage is produced through contract, legally bounded and formed. It is understood in Western democracies as a voluntary act (although marriage may limit one's freedom to commit further voluntary acts, such as resisting violence or gaining a divorce).

Nonetheless, being married is a status as well (Goldberg-Hiller 1998). Battles over same-sex marriage amount to demands for the maintenance of a certain status for heterosexuals, whether individuals choose to marry or not. This status privileges heterosexuals as part of "the founding unit of society," the reproductive family, and both relies on and maintains the exclusion of gays and lesbians from kinship. Marriage thus produces relations of status not only among the partners to the contract, and between them and their offspring, but also between them and others who are not allowed to enter into that relation and are thereby treated as promiscuous and unstable, as well as ineligible for tax relief, health insurance, inheritance, medical visitation and decision-making, and a host of other privileges conferred through marriage. Here, a particular kinship relation both is regulated by the state and confers differential citizenship rights to those who enter into it. The contrast between status and contract, so useful for the modern narrative of progress and freedom, cannot do the work of division demanded of it.

The intertwining of contract and status point to the complex ways in which public and private, citizenship and kinship work together to structure social reproduction and culture. The central role of legally recognized marriage in mediating family and state confounds modern attempts to distinguish spheres of life, whether they be community versus state, love versus justice, or any other popular contrast between the "affective" realm of family and kin-like relations and the "instrumental" realm of autonomous agents. One need not take a particular normative position on this interrelation in order to recognize its pervasiveness and its structuring role in modern Western societies. Our linguistic categories and our theories suggest that we can examine one without the other, but in fact they are always bound together. Whether in family law that prescribes forms of inheritance, obligation, and rights, or in citizenship determinations that rely on the citizen status of the parents (and most countries distinguish mothers from fathers for these purposes), kinship and citizenship work together to shape our social landscapes. These landscapes are changing as women and children gain rights within families and challenge the patriarchal rights of "the citizen." As they do so, the implicit shape of the "citizen" is becoming more clearly limned, and thus open to contestation.

Queer Families

Lesbians, gays, and bisexuals have been in the forefront of those challenging traditional family forms. As Judith Stacey (1998, 119–20) puts it, "fully intentional childbearing outside of heterosexual unions represents one of the only new, truly original, and decidedly controversial genres of family formation and structure to have emerged in the West during many centuries." Although sexual minorities are not the only people participating in this new genre, they are among the most visible and are perhaps the most troubling to advocates of traditional family arrangements.

Other non-dominant family forms, such as the extended families of many people of color and immigrants, do not present such a challenge because they generally conform to models of kinship as "natural" (i.e., not a matter of intent or cultural creation) and do not, by and large, dispute patriarchal authority. Queer families, on the other hand, challenge much more than the idea that parenthood should be available only to heterosexual married couples. They also disrupt gender norms within families, presenting the full threat of the "postmodern family condition" with "its regime of improvisation, ambiguity, diversity, contradiction, self-reflection, and flux" (Stacey 1998, 139). Thus, Stacey argues that although "gay marriage" appears to conform with hegemonic ideas about "family values," it in fact "raises far more threatening questions than does military service about gender relations, sexuality, and family life" (128).

Stacey nicely gets at the broader issue of whether "gay marriage" or "queer families" are a path toward assimilation or resistance. The answer seems to be, neither, or both. Along with other champions of families and kinship, Stacey highlights the ways in which lesbians and gays transform family structures in order to inhabit them, as well as noting the potential impact that same-sex marriage would have on anti-sodomy laws, adoption, custody, inheritance, and other family law. This is not, however, simply "resistance." Her recommendations and endorsements are not only for the ways in which sexual minorities challenge monolithic notions of "The Family," but also for the ways they creatively perform the functions of family, of social reproduction and support. Lesbian and gay families are not created de novo, from a cultural vacuum, but are bricolages of existing elements from both queer cultures and heterosexual family cultures. Given kinship's relation to citizenship, these new bricolages must be examined not only for their impact on kinship forms but also for their implications for citizenship.

As Stacey's suggestion about legal change implies, recognition of families may be used as a vehicle to citizenship; or rather, the frame of citizenship in the United States may enable sexual minority members to use kinship to gain other rights. If, for example, same-sex marriage were recognized, anti-sodomy laws would face a renewed challenge as prosecution of some forms of conjugal sex but not others would present a violation of equal protection (Stacey 1998, 128). This is not a matter of family changing citizenship, but of the conjunction of family and citizen rights being used to change law that is currently seen as not impacting on "the family."

It is not certain, however, that such a change would lead to the abolition of anti-sodomy laws. Courts might very well allow that married couples could not be restricted, while leaving sodomy between unmarried persons (either same-sex, heterosex, or other) unaffected. In the majority opinion in *Bowers v. Hardwick*, in which the Supreme Court upheld the constitutionality of sodomy laws, Justice Byron White sharply distinguished privacy concerning "child rearing and education," "family relationships," "procreation," "marriage," "contraception," and "abortion" from homosexual activity precisely as the opposition between marriage and family on the one hand and homosexuality on the other. This distinction might well shift to an opposition between "marriage and family" (whether heterosexual or not) and non-familial sex. Rather than simply leading to sexual freedom, same-sex marriage may very well intensify the line between respectable gays and lesbians and their "outlaw" cousins.

There are other questions to be asked about marriage and family. While social scientists have noted the differences between heterosexual and gay or lesbian families, much of the political activism for recognition takes the tack of arguing for the sameness of families across lines of sexual orientation. Families, according to the Lambda Legal Defense and Education Fund, should be delineated not by "blood ties or labels" but by "the quality and security of the relationship between individual children and adults" (*New York Times*, January 4, 2000, A11). This is part of a larger trajectory in political activism that denies the positioning of gays and lesbians as abject and seeks equal status as liberal subjects. As in other campaigns for equality, this approach appeals to the desires of many to belong, to be recognized as equal members of the polity and to share the rights and privileges accorded to the most advantaged of those members. Campaigns for simple equality (e.g., Sullivan 1995), however, have largely ignored the patriarchal relations of the modern heterosexual family. Taking the contemporary ideal of companionate marriage for reality, advocates argue that we should have the same rights as heterosexuals to enter into relationship. Andrew Sullivan, for example, argues that the "center" of marriage is "an emotional, financial, and psychological bond between two people" rather than a procreative contract, and that, in relation to this "public contract" of marriage, "heterosexuals and homosexuals are identical" (179). In Sullivan's world, the parties to a marriage contract are "two autonomous, independent individuals" (180); ignoring the actual history of marriage, in which women have consistently been disempowered by financial dependence and inequality, Sullivan understands marriage as the ideal liberal contract. The liberal citizen is the one who is sufficiently autonomous to enter into contractual obligation with the state, and this includes the capacity to enter into civil contracts. The autonomy that distinguishes those with the capacity for citizenship is the same autonomy that marks those capable of marriage. Consequently, Sullivan sees marriage as a good to which all citizens should have access. He cannot address the problems within existing marriages, and so can offer no guidance for how new kinship patterns might avoid them.

Even arguments that examine existing law, rather than making metaphysical assumptions as Sullivan does, can overlook the gendered hierarchical assumptions of marriage. Richard Mohr's argument for same-sex marriage (1997) includes a treatment of "gender in marital law" in which he concludes that "gender distinctions have all but vanished from the legal content of marriage" because women now have legal control over their bodies (in most states) and their property (88). Although Mohr does not claim that gender equality is the norm in fact, his argument for same-sex marriage relies partly on his claim that marriage is now a non-gendered companionate arrangement between equals. His occasional admissions that reality might be more complex are the written equivalent of mumbles—muted asides that do not really shift his attention from a narrow legal focus. His definition of marriage as "intimacy given substance in the medium of everyday life, the day-to-day" or as "the fused intersection of love's sanctity and necessity's demand" (91) downplays the inequality and subordination that are just as basic to Western marriage as and much more long-standing than, love and intimacy.

In contrast to identitarian celebratory strategies are those that claim that marriage and family are irretrievably part of what Michael Warner has called "reproculture." Warner and others have argued that reproculture is necessarily figured in heterosexual terms, and so attempts by queers to enter into reproculture's institutions will result in the "straightening" of queers. These critiques are much more sensitive to the inequalities within marriage, as well as the plurality of forms of kinship being articulated in gay and lesbian communities. They, too, however, rely on an ahistorical model of marriage. Identifying marriage with reproculture concedes the argument of the Right that marriage is justified only by procreation, an argument that is belied by the reality of current families. The increasing number of couples without children currently reside in a nebulous zone: not fully families according to kinship ideologies, they are nonetheless models of companionate liberal marriage. At least at this point in the United States, marriage and family might be seen as separate issues. And indeed, the wedge between them is the zone of greatest anxiety in debates over same-sex marriage. The gap between contractual marriage and intergenerational kinship is the gap between liberal and communitarian/conservative understandings not only of family, but of citizenship as well.

Gay and lesbian debates over marriage, exemplified by Sullivan's and Mohr's view versus that of Warner, are one site for what Urvashi Vaid (1995) has identified as the "politics of assimilation" versus "politics of resistance." In these contests, both approaches fail to sufficiently problematize the cultures they are confronting. Two questions emerge from a more nuanced portrait.

First, who exactly is the target of assimilation—that is, to whom are the mainstream thinkers and activists trying to be identical? Both sides have a narrow vision of the culture they confront. Those in favor of marriage offer a stripped-down image of America as a liberal individualist haven, in which associational freedom is basic to American identity and trumps heterosexual fears of cultural change. Queer opponents present a monolithic straight culture that hasn't changed since (pick one): the Puritans, the Victorians, the 1950s. This culture consumes anything that approaches it. If the first group suffers from an excessive abstraction of rights from their historical context, the latter relies on a caricatured context to dismiss any claims to equal rights as "straightening."

Second, what exactly is to be the same or different from the dominant group? Is there another choice, or a better way of conceptualizing sameness and difference? Kath Weston (1991) has suggested that, while gay or lesbian families aren't the same as heterosexual ones, they resemble them in important ways. She urges us to consider different family forms as commensurable rather than equivalent or the same, capable of comparison in ways that do not force one to "measure up" to the other, but instead maintain "the distinctive elements of [their] contrasting terms in the course of establishing . . . common ground" (203). Thus, for Weston kinship acts as a "bridge" concept between groups and identities often treated as discrete and opposed.

Understanding commensurability would require substantial changes in public policy. Iris Marion Young (1996, 267) has argued that "a just policy of family pluralism would consist not in the state's remaining neutral among family forms, treating them all according to the same rules no matter what their attributes, but rather would positively differentiate among some kinds of families for the sake of providing them with the support that will make them flourish equally with others." This recommendation follows from Young's more general commitment to recognizing differences and the specificities of particular situations and groups. Were we to apply this prescription to queer families, we might find a much wider challenge to reproculture than is currently evident in drives to same-sex marriage or family rights. The fact that American law and political culture are based on fierce binaries, however, makes Young's prescription one that is unlikely to be adopted anytime soon. The same thinking that has enmeshed feminists in "sameness or difference" dilemmas long past the point where the theoretical basis for this opposition became untenable makes such creative ventures in family policy inconceivable in current politics.

At this point in time it is not clear whether or in what ways alternative kinship forms are actually changing popular understandings of kinship. As Linda Nicholson (1999, ch. 3) has noted, the "traditional family" of contemporary discourse dates only to the 1950s. As divorce, remarriage, non-marriage, and same-sex households become more common, understandings have shifted to move some of these within the notion of "traditionality" without abandoning the idea of traditional families itself. As she argues, the dichotomy between "traditional" and "alternative" families continues to stigmatize certain kinds of family arrangements, reserving the privileged status of "family" for the modern quasi-nuclear family.

Against the reality of multiplicity in family forms, both anti-gay conservatives and an increasing number of lesbians and gays center "family" on reproductivity and intergenerationality. The privileged status of reproductivity supports the continued stigmatization of those, both queer and not, who pursue lives that do not include obviously procreative or reproductive elements. Ellen Lewin's research (1993) on lesbian mothers found that they, no less than their heterosexual counterparts, understood their status as mothers in terms drafted by heterosexual cultures. Lesbian mothers often expressed a belief that they were adults in a way that childless people were not, and associated motherhood with "goodness" in ways resonant of mainstream discourse (10). Lewin concludes that "like gay and lesbian marriage, the new access to traditional womanhood can divide lesbians and gays on the basis of respectability" (192). To the extent that Lewin's research still holds, it points to the migratory nature of scripts about our lives. Lewin found that the narratives of lesbian mothers were like those of heterosexual women even where their actual lives were substantially different, and these narratives contained all the traditional gender expectations and associations of motherhood that are aptly contained in the neologism of "reproculture." Consequently, Lewin warns that "the otherness of childless lesbians may be intensified not because they are lesbians but because they are not mothers" (192). Also likely to be "othered" are men and women who engage in sex outside of monogamous relationships and those who form families that are not recognizably reproductive units. Lewin's findings suggest that should the courts begin to distinguish between family and non-family queers, they would find some support among lesbians and gays as well as other Americans. This new othering must be accounted for in future arguments about the legal and social merits of marriage.

Intimate Association

In *Sexual Justice*, Morris Kaplan (1997, 238) argues both for the recognition of same-sex marriage and for the legitimation of other forms of affiliation and "erotic self-making." Kaplan, unlike Sullivan and Mohr, avoids dismissing feminist concerns about marriage even as he argues against collapsing sex equality claims with arguments for same-sex marriage (226). Kaplan frames debate in terms of "intimate association" and closely follows Justice Harry Blackmun's dissent in *Bowers* to argue for the importance of privacy rights construed not as the right to hide but as the right to affiliate. Kaplan rightly notes that "recognition and social supports are required to maintain the always precarious associations" that are so basic to human flourishing (208). He points out that same-sex marriage would amount to "acceptance of the moral legitimacy and ethical validity of the shared ways of life of lesbian and gay citizens" (209). While anti-discrimination laws are fundamentally about acceptance and "moral legitimacy," they can be distinguished from marriage in that anti-discrimination laws pertain to persons in their capacity as workers and consumers, whether of housing or services. This capacity is part of their identity as liberal citizens, which is in theory treated as distinct from their identity as family members. But, as Kaplan notes, the right to form or not form families is a part of liberal citizenship. It is also a right to a certain status, seemingly denied by liberalism yet inseparable from its history.

Kaplan's recognition of the importance of acknowledgment is part of a larger framework that links intimate association with citizenship. It thus represents a substantial advance over simple liberal arguments that structure privacy rights as a matter of being left alone (see also Boling 1996). Nonetheless, it suffers from a lack of historical and contemporary evidence about family forms and kinship ideologies. By framing the issue as one of "associational freedom," Kaplan speaks to the American courts of rights they have construed as basic. Intimate association, however, will not necessarily overcome the residues of status distinction embedded in marriage. Recent developments indicate that some courts are able to support equality and intimate association without recognizing, much less finding invalid, the privilege of heterosexual marriage.

Kaplan argues that those who fear assimilation and "the imitation of heterosexist models" both underestimate and exaggerate the importance of legal rights (1997, 226). Legal recognition creates the space for creating new institutions. Forced acknowledgment of same-sex marriage will eventually result in changed attitudes. On the other hand, recognition enables individuals to imagine new ways of doing things; including queers in marriage does not mean that we will passively fit into existing forms, but opens the possibility for revisioning marriage in ways more resonant for our lives and communities. I agree with him about the possibilities that arise in such situations, but reading recent work such as Lewin's makes me pessimistic about the actual direction of change here. Kaplan's focus on legal and philosophical argument produces a cogent analysis that is not borne out by either current ethnography or the aftermath of partnership legislation in Scandinavia. Rune Halvorsen's examination (1998) of the Norwegian Registered Partnership Act, for example, finds that even the "symbolic effect" of the Act has been less than either opponents or proponents expected. The battle over the legislation made clear that, in Norway at least, there exists a hierarchy of kinship forms with heterosexual marriage at the peak: opponents supported legislation that would recognize and regulate partnerships on the same terms as cohabitating couples, friends, or siblings (210–11). The explicit denial of religious ceremony and the abbreviated civil ceremony, as well as the explicit denial of adoption rights, continued to mark a distinction between marriage and all other forms. Likewise, the recent Vermont Supreme Court decision that found that denial of same-sex partnership (in some form) was a violation of that state's constitutional requirement of equality led immediately to attempts to conform to the decision without actually allowing marriage on a par with opposite-sex marriage. The commitment to equality rarely goes so far as to allow that our kinship forms deserve the acknowledgment given to heterosexual marriage.

Halvorsen notes that the battle over partnership is partly over liberal individualist versus communalist visions of the polity. While "relationships and sexual relations have increasingly become regarded as a private matter and as dependent on how well the people involved fit together as personalities," parenthood "is widely regarded as a different thing" (1998, 225). Conceptions of sexual love have enabled many people to admit the liberal principle that adults should be able to make their own civil associations, but this conception has not, in Norway at least—and, I would argue, elsewhere—significantly changed prevailing views about kinship and family. Instead of contrasting the unaffiliated queer with the heterosexual family, liberal debates have shifted to contrasting couples and families. Couples without children are treated as less mature, less rooted (note the link between the two latter terms) than those with children. Just as Lewin's lesbian mothers looked down on their childless friends, the Norwegian experience documents the privilege of intergenerational families and the simultaneous attempt to bar lesbians and gays from participating in them.

Of course Kaplan is not suggesting that recognition be limited in the ways embodied in the Norwegian partnership act: the distinction between marriage and partnership, as well as the ban on adoption, for him would surely smack of continued discrimination. Nonetheless, the Norwegian experience is helpful in clarifying the gaps between legal and social recognition and between marriage and family. Kaplan's argument for associational freedom addresses the right to marry, but the Norwegian case suggests that the issue is not only one of personal freedom but also of social symbolic recognition. If kinship retains its priority in structuring and imaging the polity, and if the "pure relationship" is detached from kinship, then marriage alone will not address our exclusion. Nor, for that matter, will the inclusion of lesbian or gay families with children. They will more likely appear to the heterosexual majority as a mere copy of the "real thing," the generative heterosexual couple.

This does not mean that there is no hope for change. Changes in families may lead to changes in citizenship, as "we're like you" moves to "we resemble you." Social recognition of diverse kinship relations may also provide the basis for new challenges to the link between family status and citizenship. As gay, bisexual, and lesbian families continue to develop and to emerge in public, we may hope that their different daily reality will lead to changes in the narratives of that reality. The possible scope and extent of these changes will depend partly upon the particular racial and gendered forms of kinship and citizenship a given community holds. Efforts to include same-sex marriage that do not address the gendered structure of marriage or its function in maintaining racial divisions will succeed at most in winning "equality" for a privileged sector of white well-off (not-so) queers.

If we do not fear the normalizing impulse of family, we may have other concerns about the heightened focus on family among gays and lesbians. While masculinist thinkers have treated families as the "training ground of citizenship," our first school in ethics and human relations, we may find instead that citizenship is endangered by familism and reproculture. Although advocates such as O'Neill make a case for family's ability to provide resources of resistance, they may unwittingly substitute an ideal family for actual families in contemporary capitalist societies. To the extent that "family" is understood as a zone of natural relations and privacy from the public or the state, its celebration serves the needs of capital rather than those of citizens. Rights then become a means to private life and citizenship is understood as the equal right to pursuit of private life, exempt from critical scrutiny. This is not a problem of assimilation per se, of becoming "like" heterosexual families and abandoning what is distinctive about queer cultures, but is a result of participation in wider modern dilemmas of citizenship. Just as Lewin found that lesbian mothers recite from scripts that do not reflect their lives, it is possible for those of us who are not mothers or fathers, or husbands or wives, to recite from the scripts that make these relations the acme of human aspiration and desire. I am saying, though, that currently LGBT communities offer more access to alternative narratives than do heterosexual ones. Losing that access would represent a loss, not only for sexual minorities but for others who want to envision other forms of adhesion and affiliation.

The gravest danger in the push for wider recognition of diverse families lies in naturalizing or reifying new kinship patterns. Such naturalizing prevents us from examining the relations between the state and kinship. The belief that we form families and ask only for state recognition maintains the liberal fiction of autonomous subjects in civil society. Even as they form the basis for activism, Anglo-American narratives of kinship consistently lead us away from political engagement and understanding of the interrelation between citizenship and kinship. To make expanded notions of family an element of citizenship we must work simultaneously to break the high walls separating family from state in dominant ideologies. States are central actors in the construction and maintenance of modern families, but popular narratives obscure this reality. Rather than grafting our lives onto existing ideas about family and kinship and their opposition to political relations, those concerned for democratic citizenship should actively seek to transform our ideas, our institutions, and our policies in order to provide the conditions for families that do in fact raise children to be participatory, equal citizens and that support connections between adults.

Negotiating Strangeness

Assimilation and Visibility

escribing the dilemma of Jewish refugees from Nazism, Hannah Arendt constructs a composite "Mr. Cohn from Berlin," a man who "had always been a 150% German, a German super-patriot" (Arendt 1978, 62). Upon the Nazi rise to power, Mr. Cohn, if he saw clearly, left and went somewhere else. Upon arrival he became a patriot of whatever country he landed in. When the Nazis pressured the government of his new land, or invaded, he left and found another "home." What Mr. Cohn cannot bear, cannot face, according to Arendt, is the fact that for these governments and their Christian populations, he is never a German, or a Czech, or a Frenchman, or an American; he is a Jew.

Arendt is sympathetic to Mr. Cohn's urge and his fear even as she criticizes them. She cautions that

> if we should start telling the truth that we are nothing but Jews,
> it would mean that we expose ourselves to the fate of human
> beings who, unprotected by any specific law or political
> convention, are nothing but human beings. I can hardly imagine
> an attitude more dangerous, since we actually live in a world in
> which human beings as such have ceased to exist for quite a
> while; since society has discovered discrimination as the great
> social weapon by which one may kill men without any
> bloodshed. (65)

Mr. Cohn's dilemma is recognizable not only to other Jews or other refugees, but to many of those who become strangers. Being "nothing but human beings" in a world carefully regulated by regimes of nationality, gender, race, sexuality, and class does not invite an appeal to universal standards of decency but rather disassociation and denial of equality. The history of the twentieth century makes clear that "human beings" do not have standing in politics (Arendt 1966, 267–302). In order to challenge injustice and claim decent treatment, one must be recognized as a member of the polity being challenged.

Like the refugee, strangers are faced with a dilemma. Do they insist on their earlier ways of life while claiming legal inclusion and protection, or do they try to become "150% German" (or American, Canadian, Russian, Israeli . . .)? It seems that neither choice alone is sufficient. Allegiances might shift, but language and culture are not immediately pliable. Liberal regimes promise that one can retain one's culture and language as "private" matters while participating in legal and political affairs as a generic citizen. Any stranger who enters such a regime, however, becomes closely attuned to the ways in which such liberal regimes presume cultural norms that they cannot avow as such. Strangers who grow up in the midst of regimes, who do not know they are strangers until they are adolescent or older, may be less sharply attuned to cultural presumptions. It is likely that they will discover those that stigmatize and reject them prima facie, but the relation between the prima facie exclusions and more subtle cultural injunctions may be less clear.

Identifying the range of injunctions and norms does not guarantee their rejection. One of the major avenues of cultural change and creativity lies in the refusal of individuals and groups to read their culture as they are told they must. Famously, the Reformation carved a new road between individual faith in a Christian God and obedience to secular and religious human authority. Civil rights movements have adapted the language of liberal individualism, turning it to uses that its authors did not intend (Forment 1995; Williams 1991). Strangers, like other excluded groups, are likely to share some norms with those who exclude them; this is especially likely for sexual strangers whose "home" culture is the one that rejects them.

We should not then be surprised when sexual strangers try to (re)gain membership. Nor should it raise eyebrows when sexual strangers approach membership by making claims to be "150% American." Correctly identifying the core values of American political culture, gays and lesbians in particular have sought "a place at the table" (Bawer 1993) by staking claim to superior citizen virtues. Like creative social movements before them, sexual minority activists have worked both to reject earlier views and to claim them.

We are currently witnessing the growth of diverse arguments and strategies for confronting and overcoming sexual strangeness. This growth is both a result and an instigator of changes in the acceptability of sexual minorities in the United States. As Cathy Cohen (1999) notes, marginalization is not a singular, static process, but is "dialectical" and dynamic. Cohen usefully distinguishes what she calls "categorical exclusion" from "integrative marginalization," in which general exclusion coexists with "limited mobility of some 'deserving' marginal group members" (26). The latter eventually gives way to "advanced marginalization," characterized by the combination of limited mobility and "direct management of other, less privileged marginal group members" to more privileged group members—self-policing. Thus, advanced marginalization necessitates "secondary marginalization," in which group elites invoke "a rhetoric of blame and punishment" toward the most stigmatized group members (27). Secondary marginalization occurs precisely at the point where an end to marginalization appears to be just around the corner. The dominant regime's patterns of speech, bodily comportment, and consciousness become more attractive, more "natural," at this point for those who can achieve them. At the stage of advanced marginalization, elites are caught between their desire to be treated as "individuals" or "Americans" and their continuing reassignment to stigmatized group membership. Thus, the deviation of some from dominant norms becomes especially frustrating; every time "they" misbehave, "we" all suffer!

The costs of advanced and secondary marginalization are intertwined with the benefits that acceptance promises. In this chapter I examine one current path to citizenship, what I will call the "new gay visibility" in mainstream politics and public discourse. Specifically, I focus on the attempt to assimilate gays and lesbians into American society by demonstrating their fundamental normality. This attempt is an inevitable response to strangeness, but it is flawed for two reasons. First, it underestimates the depth and extent of rejection faced by sexual strangers, a rejection that is not only intellectual or dogmatic, but extends for many to visceral revulsion. Second, the cost of assimilatory projects is the reinforcement of binary structures of gender and kinship that are fundamental to the maintenance and proliferation of sexual strangers. I thus argue that although the new gay visibility represents a significant advance for gays and lesbians in the United States, it also creates new binaries and new exclusions. It may be that this is the price of any new inclusion in modernity; if this is so, however, that price must be acknowledged as the exclusion and rejection of actual persons.

Assimilation and Its Discontents

Assimilation of "foreigners" has always been a salient issue in politics. The Greeks debated whether and how foreigners could become citizens. Rome's imperial structure, like that of empires before and after it, required a subtle negotiation between leaving "the locals" their culture and importing enough Roman culture to ensure that its rule seemed justified. Modernity, however, has exacerbated the problem of assimilation. In regimes where nationality and territorial borders are "supposed" to coincide, those who belong somewhere else pose a problem. Worse, however, is the dilemma presented by those who don't belong in that nation-state, and yet don't belong in any other either. This is most acute for those "foreigners" who were born and raised in the country that rejects them. For decades the children of Turkish workers in Germany have been denied German citizenship, yet they have never been to Turkey, speak fluent German, and go to German schools. Throughout modernity, Jews have been treated as residents of nations rather than cultural citizens and have engaged in painful debates about the costs and benefits of assimilation.

Debates over the membership of such groups have outlined the issues at stake for most strangers, even if the nuances of these issues differ according to the specific position(s) of the group. These debates take place both among the strangers and among the dominant population, but here my concern is with those who are excluded. The first question is, what are the benefits of assimilating—what is to be gained by inclusion in the national identity? Second, what are the costs—what will be lost, either in cultural integrity, intragroup relations, or otherwise? Third, how should assimilation be achieved? As a part of this third, but perhaps also the primary question, is assimilation possible at all? Does the regime admit of the sort of flexibility that would enable creative re-formation of national identities?

Perhaps surprisingly, in the United States assimilation has come to be a term of disdain. In a country that prided itself on its success at assimilating masses of new people from diverse origins, fights for cultural recognition and identity politics have made assimilation suspect precisely to those who might seek it, while the hegemonic ideology continues to revere its promise of equality. In contrast to generations of immigrants who strove to assimilate, currently even gay Republicans such as Richard Tafel reject assimilation as a goal. Tafel characterizes assimilationism as a "therapeutic" response to rejection, aiming at inclusion on any terms available (Tafel 1999, 30–34). Tafel characterizes his own view as "libertarian," a matter of seeing oneself as "a complex individual whose sexual orientation is but one facet of his life, and rarely the most important one. He believes he is personally responsible for his own successes and failures" (49). While Tafel's opponents might justifiably argue that such a view is already assimilated, what is striking here is that this grandson of German immigrants who inveighs against identity politics nonetheless rejects assimilation. Assimilation, like essentialism, is an idea with no adherents but many accusers.

Recent work on assimilation, however, may shed some light on this curiosity. Bauman (1991, 103) points out that "assimilation" was first used in English to describe the biological phenomenon whereby an organism incorporated and absorbed other organisms. The term's biological basis made for convenient translation into discussion of bodies social and political. Assimilation, whether organic or political, was not a process initiated or even chosen by the assimilated, but rather by the larger body. We must remember at the outset, then, that assimilation is not the choice of the stigmatized, but of the powerful. And the larger body assimilates lesser ones not for the good of the lesser, but for its own goals.

Liberal regimes often reverse this understanding, portraying assimilation as the project of individuals or groups who wish to join the larger group. This reversal obscures the agency of the dominant and takes their culture and standing for granted. The burden of assimilation rests on what is outside and wants to be in. The specific weight of the burden is the demand to become culturally assimilable, combined with group stigma that ensures that satisfaction of the demand can fail at any time (Bauman 1991, 69–78; Rubin 1995). Unlike the citizens of liberal theory, who "are entitled to respect unless they forfeit it by their own unacceptable actions" (Shklar 1991, 2–3), strangers are judged by both their own actions and those of other strangers.

Rather than ameliorating inequality, then, assimilation reinforces and perpetuates it. Assimilatory projects strengthen the dominant group's belief that they are desirable: "the more you are like me, the more I know the true value of my power, which you wish to share, and the more I am aware that you are but a shoddy counterfeit, an outsider" (Gilman 1985, 2). This does not mean that dominant cultures are never transformed by encounters with other ideas or ways of life. The presence and prominence of those currently or formerly marked "other" in political or cultural life, as well as the wide popularity of foods, fashions, and musics that combine and adapt diverse elements of the cultures of "others" argues against such a stark proposition. The most optimistic political theorists on this issue not implausibly read some assimilation as the new interpellation of strangers as citizens as well as the re-interpellation of existing citizens (see, e.g., Kaplan 1997). The inequality of assimilation does mean, however, that the onus of change is more likely to be placed on strangers than on "natives." The claim of recognition does not occur within a liberal situation of equality or "veil of ignorance," but within pre-existing networks of cultural power and meaning. Thus recognition may be offered by dominant members to the extent that strangers "take on mainstream cultural practices," even though liberal theory and stated liberal constitutionalism do not demand it (Spinner 1994, 7). Citizenship is more than theory and constitution, however. The acknowledgment that is its sine qua non requires that one be recognized as being "like" existing members in some ways. The centrality of bodily and discursive comportment and kinship practices to citizenship points to their importance in attempts at assimilation. Those who seek entry will be pressured to adopt dominant norms in these arenas as the price of admission.

Such adoption may not seem onerous to many, as some strangers "may have cultural practices similar to those of their oppressors" (Spinner 1994, 24–25). But the processes of advanced marginalization lead those individuals to compel assimilation by other group members as well. It is not enough to be a "good homosexual" oneself (Smith 1994a); one needs all the others to be good as well if one is to solidify one's status. As we will see, much recent gay writing follows the pattern of appealing to heterosexuals for acceptance while castigating sexual minorities for their violations of dominant gender and sexual codes. This is not incidental, a failure of particular individuals, but is a necessity built into the structure of strangeness. Assimilation is doomed to be attempted, and to fail, as long as strangeness persists.

In *Justice and the Politics of Difference,* Iris Marion Young (1990, ch. 5) describes how groups may simultaneously confront what she labels conscious acceptance and unconscious aversion. Following Anthony Giddens, Young distinguishes between "discursive consciousness, practical consciousness, and a basic security system" (131). Discursive consciousness is distinguished from practical consciousness in that the former can be verbalized and is available to conscious reflection and discussion, while the latter is the habitual, routinized background awareness that enables persons to accomplish focused, immediately purposive action" (131). The basic security system consists of the most elementary level of security and sense of self. All of these levels respond to and enact conceptions of identity, order, and danger.

Civil rights struggles primarily, and necessarily, concern themselves with the level of discursive consciousness. In discussions with legislators, the media, and the public, gay and lesbian rights activists address arguments that would deny equality to sexual minorities. However, they well know that legislative decisions are not made only at the level of discursive consciousness; unconscious aversion works to block arguments as powerfully as does logic. Many marginalized people have experienced the moment when a "normal" person voices support, even acts on the principle of equality, yet clearly manifests personal discomfort or revulsion for members of the stigmatized group. Often these two gestures are combined by distinguishing between the "good" (i.e., respectable) and "bad" members of the stigmatized group. Pushy Jews, dirty immigrants, and lazy blacks join the flaming queen and the mannish lesbian in this category (see, e.g., Smith 1994a). This is part of the reason why leaders have insisted on "respectable" dress and behavior and have sought heroes among the most normal of queers. As Marshall Kirk and Hunter Madsen argued in 1989, an effective movement for equality could not simply thumb its nose at all the conventions of the powerful and hope for success. In so doing, Kirk and Madsen echoed Young's caution that "assimilation into the dominant culture, acceptance into the rosters of relative privilege, requires that members of formerly excluded groups adopt professional postures and suppress the expressiveness of their bodies" (Young 1990, 140).

Young identifies the demand for respectability as an injustice in itself. She recognizes the differential burden put upon oppressed groups who must police their own members. If such groups fail to challenge the demand for respectability, their attempts at social change will operate only at the more superficial levels of discursive consciousness without transforming the more basic structures of identity that shape our reactions to the world. This demand, however, is almost impossible to resist. For strangers seeking entry, respectability may not seem a burden at all, but rather an invitation to norms already held by many group members. This is likely to be especially true for sexual strangers, who grow up in the same communities that mark them as strange. It is especially the case for leaders, what Erving Goffman (1963, 26) calls "professional stigma representatives," who in their dealings with other groups "so find themselves breaking out of the closed circle of their own kind . . . ceasing, in terms of social participation, to be representative of the people they represent." Such leaders are likely to succeed precisely to the extent to which they challenge intragroup norms and ally themselves with dominant standards of dress, comportment, and ideas. As we will see, sexual strangers are no exception to this pattern.

The New Gay Discourse

The 1990s produced unprecedented visibility for sexual minorities, and with it a proliferation of perspectives, venues, and modes of entry into U.S. social and political institutions. The AIDS crisis of the 1980s and 1990s funneled people whose political agendas and social views are substantially different from earlier activists. Increased public tolerance (itself the result of earlier organizing) made it possible for many to come out and maintain their standards of living. The sharp increase in participation and agenda-setting by middle-class, well-educated, relatively conservative white men has led to new groups targeted on electoral politics, more funding for mainstream organizations, and more ideological diversity among gay and lesbian organizations (Epstein 1999; Rayside 1998, ch. 9). Although gay and lesbian political organizations have existed for decades, it was not until the 1990s that national organizations resembling other interest-group organizations began to form. The National Gay and Lesbian Task Force (NGLTF), active since the 1970s, has always suffered from funding and membership limitations. Now, the Human Rights Campaign (HRC) maintains a full-time lobbying and fund-raising staff; and the Gay and Lesbian Victory Fund, established to support lesbian and gay political candidates, has been very successful in a short period of time (Rimmerman 1996). Both these organizations and their leaders, as well as other anointed gay leaders who can be counted on for sound bites, " have become visible to an extent hard to imagine even ten years ago. Surely to many lesbians and gays, and certainly to their strongest opponents, America has been won by the forces of Sodom.

This growth in acceptability, along with the commitment of well-off educated gays and lesbians, has provided an atmosphere for public discussions of lesbian and gay politics and culture. These discussions have taken shape both "inside" communities and "outside" them, as the mass media has discovered a new hot topic. During the 1990s, lesbians were featured in cover stories for *Time* and *Newsweek;* sitcom star Ellen DeGeneres and her character both "came out" to America; and Andrew Sullivan, former editor of the *New Republic,* came out in print and to date has published three books on homosexual politics. These are only the most prominent moments in a seemingly unending wave of mass-market books, magazines, and television programs.

Until 1989, very little gay and lesbian writing was published by major publishing houses with the resources to produce and advertise on a large scale. That year saw the beginnings of the shift with Marshall Kirk and Hunter Madsen's *After the Ball.* Although this book was addressed primarily to gays rather than to non-gays (including lesbians), its publication by Doubleday and coverage in *Newsweek,* the *Washington Post,* and other mainstream media gave it a publicity lacking to any other gay/lesbian non-fiction, non-autobiographical book in recent history; indeed, the *Indianapolis News* stated that the book "should be read by almost everyone in American society" (Kirk and Madsen, 1989). Since 1990 the development of a mass market for gay and lesbian books has led to volumes by, among others, David Mixner (activist and erstwhile friend of President Clinton), Candace Gingrich (sister of the former Republican Speaker of the House, now a staffer for the Human Rights Campaign), Richard Tafel (executive director of Log Cabin Republicans, a gay group), Torie Osborne (former executive director of the National Gay and Lesbian Task Force), Urvashi Vaid (likewise), Gabriel Rotello (journalist and AIDS activist), Michelangelo Signorile (likewise), Margarethe Cammermeyer (armed service member discharged for lesbianism), Joseph Steffan (armed service member discharged for being gay), and Greg Louganis (Olympic swimmer).

The boom has included the publication of three books explicitly arguing for lesbian and gay political equality: Michael Nava and Robert Dawidoff's *Created Equal: Why Gay Rights Matter to America* (St. Martin's Press, 1993); Richard Mohr's *A More Perfect Union: Why Straight America Must Stand Up for Gay Rights* (Beacon Press, 1994); and Andrew Sullivan's *Virtually Normal: An Argument about Homosexuality* (Knopf, 1995).[1]

We may say that with these books and activities gays (and, to a much lesser extent, lesbians) have begun to enter the mainstream of American public life. Of course, lesbians and gays have been engaging in public action for decades, but their efforts have largely met with silence rather than debate. These activities facilitated discussion and connection among lesbians and gays, but until recently there were few concerted attempts to persuade heterosexuals of the injustice of heterosexism. With the new books and mainstream political activity, lesbians and gays are intervening in arguments that have too often either ignored them or treated them as the objects of majority disposition.

This new intervention presents a major shift in gay and lesbian politics. As Seyla Benhabib (1992, 79) has noted, "the struggle over what gets included in the public agenda is itself a struggle for justice and freedom." The line between public and private is a shifting one whose boundaries are always fraught with multiple meanings. In liberal discourse, the "private" has been both a zone of protection and a domain of inequality and domination (Boling 1996). Conversely, publicity has carried multiple meanings. "The public" has been understood to be a space of equality, rationality (and, in liberal thought, disembodied neutrality), a space in which citizens gather to meet and deliberate. It is, as

Michael Warner (1993) reminds us, a space both of presence and of disembodiment, for

> the rhetorical strategy of personal abstraction is both the utopian moment
> of the public sphere and a major source of domination. For the ability to
> abstract oneself in public discussion has always been an unequally available
> resource. Individuals have to have specific rhetorics of disincorporation; they
> are not simply rendered bodiless by exercising reason. And it is only possible
> to operate a discourse based on the claim to self- abstracting disinterested-
> ness in a culture where such unmarked self-abstraction is a differential
> resource. (239)

For those living with stigma, on the other hand, "publicity" has also
meant exposure and shame and has been a weapon as much as a promise; as Patricia Boling (1994) has noted in her discussion of outing,
unwelcome publicity is not an entry into equal citizenship so much as
it is a punishment and another, glaring, isolation. Stigma's articulation
through embodiment makes the quest for visibility a wildly paradoxical one; being public, especially as a sexual minority, always invites
embarrassment as well as pride.

The dilemma of publicity, in which equality and exposure are twins,
is acute for sexual minorities. Its recent resolutions (which are not resolutions but shifting accommodations) have had two predominant shapes.
The first, "queer" response has been to refuse the shame of homosexuality by being as visible as possible, not simply as a neutral body marked
"homosexual" but as flaming, screaming, butch or femme—revealing
the twists of gender and sexuality that seem to induce the greatest discomfort among straights (of whatever sexual orientation). This response
will be discussed later in this chapter. I will focus first on the second
response, manifested in virtually all of the new "mainstream" books,
which asserts equality and encourages the individual visibility of gay
men and lesbians in order to demonstrate their normality. This visibility, however, must be carefully managed in order to be both abstract
(i.e., appropriate to the public) and concrete. Homosexuality becomes
visible solely as a category of identity, a category that leads some to
oppress others. Thus "public" homosexuality consists of statements—
"I am a lesbian"—that are simultaneously abstract and pointing to an
embodied way of life. Assimilationist visibility in politics becomes a
matter of saying without doing. I am not suggesting that no division
between public and private is legitimate. Reserving aspects of our lives

for ourselves and our intimates is a crucial part of freedom. In its failure to interrogate existing zones of privacy, however, the new gay discourse fails to address the concerns of women (of all sexualities) and children, as well as those of many men, about how "privacy" continues to limit our ability to question and change injustice.

Rather than confronting dominant understandings of gender, sexuality, and the state, as well as the fears based on those understandings, the new gay discourse rests on a blend of liberal political principles and appeals to empathy.[2] Most of the new books are distinguished by their clear address of heterosexuals. Where most earlier books assumed a gay or lesbian audience and discussed issues within those communities, the new gay discourse does not. The necessity to speak to an audience that might not want to listen generates a dialectic in these works that is perhaps inevitable in liberal societies: the dialectic between personal pain and liberal principles. These authors hope that this dialectic will produce not only liberty but belonging: "coming home to America," "a place at the table," "a more perfect union," where all are "created equal." The principles of liberalism are not enough for citizenship; virtually all of these new books lay claim to membership as well.

These new books walk a line between equality and inequality in their address. They overtly plead to the powerful—in fact, Mohr and Nava and Dawidoff state this intent in their subtitles. At the same time, however, all purport to speak in the classic style of the bourgeois public: reasonably, man to man, as it were. They do not assume larger social equality, but they treat their readers as earnest citizens with whom one may deliberate calmly and overcome prejudice. "Without too much effort," Mohr assures us in *Gays/Justice* (1988), the more academic precursor to *A More Perfect Union*, "gays can generate the right sort of arguments, ones that appeal to broad principle and avoid the taunt of 'special interest group'" (329). He recommends the development of such arguments as an alternative to "bothering too much about building coalitions" (329), although he is not clear about the reason for the exclusivity of these options: either he presumes that coalitions seem too much like interest groups, or he believes that without the arguments any coalition is unreliable, but he does not make his position clear. What is clear is his philosopher's faith in the power of reason, even between clearly unequal parties. Such faith, however, can only be justified by demonstrating that such arguments have in the past served to convince oppressors to cease their oppression. Such demonstrations are not impossible to offer, but they remain rare enough to be a flimsy support for such faith.

In order for their arguments to succeed, authors in this vein must establish their humanity before those who might be presumed to question it. This gives rise to the strategy of credentialing by pain, even to open very abstract arguments. Sullivan opens his book by describing his childhood awkwardness and isolation; Bawer describes the anxiety of a teen-age boy he sees in a bookstore in Manhattan; Mohr opens with a brief description of harassment by local boys while out with his lover. Each of these attempts to "put a human face" on a social problem is, not coincidentally, accomplished through the sharing of pain. Pain establishes not only that the author knows whereof he speaks; it also appeals to the heterosexual reader who thinks of homosexuals as "them."

The second strategy, also inevitable in assimilationist projects, is the construction of the group as normal by condemning the less assimilated among the group. Not all of these books do this equally, and some do not do it at all. For Kirk and Madsen, conformity seems not to be a principled position but a marketing strategy. For others, such as Sullivan and Bawer, this is not a cynical move to buy acceptance by sacrificing "our own," but rather a manifestation of real principled differences and perspectives among a diverse group. It is nonetheless important to consider the consequences of hailing a "silent majority" of gays who hate the gay and lesbian movement and activists and who conform to gender and sexual norms (Bawer 1993, 26). It is easy for such writers to turn from the project of argument with heterosexuals toward castigation of their comrades; if you would just act less queer, say Bawer, Sullivan, Kirk, and Madsen, we'd be accepted as normal. Even as they condemn homophobia, they suppose that queerness (not homosexuality) is the problem. In their bid to be good enough, they isolate themselves from any others still marked "other." Bids for membership on the part of strangers require such a maneuver; the quest for "de-estrangement" leads strangers to "reaffirm the inferiority, undesirability, and out-of-placeness of the stranger's form of life," to accept that the burden of guilt is theirs, as is the burden of proving "entitlement to absolution" (Bauman 1991, 71).

A striking example of this is Sullivan's claim that gender non-conformity is not a legitimate difference, but rather the residue of oppression. Although Sullivan seems to celebrate gayness in the final chapter of his book, he joins the litany of those who find that mannerisms, dress, and careers that violate expectations are the product of oppression rather than valuable creations and revolts: "Once I found the strength to be myself" after coming out, he writes, "I had no need to act myself. So my clothes became progressively more regular and slovenly; I lost interest in drama; my writing moved from fiction to journalism; my speech gradually became less affected" (199). Sullivan is arguing that his assimilated heterosexual gay self is his "real" self, not "affected" as was his oppressed gay self. As a result, he reconsolidates rather than loosens the current hegemonic formulation of gender and sexuality. Men are men, women are women, and other spaces are the unfortunate byproducts of prohibition.

We need not conclude from the above that all public gay or lesbian discourse must reinforce prevailing gender, racial, and sexual norms. The year 1995 also witnessed the publication of Urvashi Vaid's *Virtual Equality*. In contrast to Sullivan, whose use of "virtual" indicates his belief that homosexuals are really just about normal, Vaid draws on the sense of virtual as apparent as in "virtual reality." Her critique of "the mainstreaming of gay and lesbian liberation" is written both to lesbians and gays concerned about the status of the movement for equality and to heterosexuals interested in political processes.

For Vaid, equality for gays and lesbians is not matter of legitimation by heterosexuals upon adoption of their norms. Equality requires both rights against discrimination, what she labels "civil equality," and the recognition of features and qualities not unique to lesbians and gays but formulated in specific forms in our many communities. She sums this up as the principles of "gay and lesbian morality": "a commitment to honesty, demonstrated by the experience of coming out; a commitment to community, or a love that surpasses the definition of family and relationship we inherited from the heterosexual norm; and a commitment to joy, expressed in our affirmation of pleasure, both sexual and nonsexual" (380). In this formulation Vaid expresses what might be understood as the principles guiding one particular counterpublic. Because that public is not enclaved, these principles are also offered as potentially available to others. They do not represent her list of how to be queer, or what queers are really like, but rather her answer to Sullivan's question, What are homosexuals for? What might the distinct experiences and institutions of queer life offer to us and to others? Here queer distinctiveness is not simply a product of oppression, but represents the possibility of real transformation through the intersection of and communication between counterpublics. Clearly this communication will be conflictual, for many do not value the three commitments offered. Still, or perhaps because of that, the articulation of the value of a queer way of life is a stronger contribution to social diversity and change than is the plea of sameness.

Another strength of Vaid's approach is her frank recognition that lesbians and gays differ among ourselves politically, and her refusal to rule out of bounds any group. She is clear that "the gay community" is already many publics, and she urges us to learn how to fight well rather than attempt to silence the parts that do not fit any one image. Thus she does not abandon gay conservatives as they abandon her (or attempt to: they cannot control the associations made by others, hard as they try). While she argues, she does not assume that politics is a matter simply of arguments.

There are several possible explanations that we might offer for Vaid's exceptional intervention into the new gay discourse. Is it relevant that she is a woman of color? Probably. She says, "I will never be convinced that racial and gender issues belong in some 'other' movement; they are fused in my body with my lesbianism, and I reject single identity-based politics" (376). But perhaps just as important is the fact that she writes as an experienced lawyer and political worker. She knows far better than professional philosophers or writers (including this one) the reality of conflicting publics and the need to balance conflict and cooperation. She also knows the limits of argument, but she does not reject argument as a central element of change.

In the end it does not matter why Vaid offers a better public vision than the authors of the new gay discourse. Public realms do highlight argument, and the argument and vision she offers matter more than any diagnosis of her ability to offer it.

Vaid embraces the diversity of queer identities and the distinct spaces created for the formation and re-formation of those identities, but she challenges the idea that these spaces are ever fully adequate for either self-expression or political activism. She rejects the idea that gay and lesbian liberation is a matter simply of equality for those born different. Although she strongly emphasizes the importance of fighting for those who experience themselves this way, she rejects strategies that tend toward a collapse into single-issue identity politics (289). This rejection is itself in accord with a public vision in which counterpublics are not enclaves but continually changing zones of political discussion and identification.

Media Savvy: The Closeting of Butch Lesbians

As an example of the ways in which the new gay visibility sacrifices gender nonconformists in order to win mainstream acceptance, I turn here to the (non)portrayal of butch lesbians in both homosexual and heterosexual assertions of equality. Butchness is imbricated in the same performative fabric within which late moderns of every stripe negotiate their lives; it is neither the expression of a true essence, nor a voluntary performance," nor a compulsory production. It is a mode of being in modern Western societies that is consistently contentious. Recent gay rights activism and discourse intervenes in that contention by its determination not to present butch lesbian images to the heterosexual public. In this, it sharply limits the possibilities and demands of queer peoples.

The new closeting of butches has not been overtly argued and justified (or thoroughly contested) by any public discussion. Although lesbian communities have debated and continue to debate butch and femme as modes of being, this debate has not seeped into mainstream gay and lesbian politics. Rather, the new closeting has followed from the adoption of mainstream political, media, and corporate tactics and goals. When challenging exclusion, lesbians and gays have largely erased the fact of their bodies and their desires. Rather than confront the dominant desire and its concomitant fears, "public" lesbians have downplayed the existence of alternative, potentially more challenging, aesthetics. This strategy is a mistake. The shift to disembodied lesbianism as a status bereft of cultural significance is an effort to be accepted by mainstream America, but the price of success is the abandonment of the most visible and vulnerable lesbians.

Although the rhetoric of contemporary social movements has thoroughly incorporated the metaphors of visibility, erasure, and closeting as central to questions of oppression and freedom, a critique of strategies of closeting must begin with a new understanding of "the closet." The closet never fully conceals; rather, it acts as a screen through which certain elements are partially visible, simultaneously serving as the surface for projections. This dual screening is what Maria Lugones and Elizabeth Spelman (1983) label "cultural imperialism." As Iris Young explains, cultural imperialistic practices "render the particular perspective of one's own group invisible at the same time as they stereotype one's group and mark it out as the other" (Young 1990, 58–59). Thus, the closet as screen does not simply hide or conceal "reality"; rather, it is the space within which and upon which hegemonic understandings are projected. From this understanding, we can refigure visibility and erasure not as questions of the faithful presentation or covering up of authentic lives, but as opportunities for more varied descriptions of lesbian lives. Far from being a seamless unity, lesbian existence opens up a multitude of paths and decisions. Erasure removes the variety of lesbians from public view, thus colluding in homophobic anxieties by maintaining dominant stereotypes.

Responses to erasure have long been contested within lesbian communities. How particular communities respond reflects the situations they encounter, and their responses in turn structure new situations. This is evident in the history of controversy over butch lesbians. Scholars such as Elizabeth Kennedy and Madeline Davis (1993) have documented conflicts concerning butches in the 1950s. In the Buffalo, New York, lesbian communities that they studied, Kennedy and Davis found that although butch/femme served as both a powerful personal code of behavior and as an "organising principle for community life," there was nonetheless contest over roles (152). They argue that the primary dividing line between those who muted their butchness or their lesbianism and those who did not was drawn by class. Improved economic opportunities after World War II enabled out butches to find blue-collar work at the same time as it opened the possibility of upward mobility for those who were willing and able to be "discreet" (145). Thus two fundamentally different paths opened for lesbians. The first encouraged working-class butches to live without the demands of passing, and enabled femmes to more easily live with butches as they chose. The second path led to a muting of butch/femme, most conspicuously to a call for butches to be less "obvious."

Lesbians who wanted acceptance from middle-class individuals and organizations wrestled with just what that acceptance required. In the 1950s the predominant paradigm of homosexuality remained the sexological conception of "sexual inversion," in which it was understood that the "true" lesbian desired women because psychically she had not reconciled herself to femininity. Sexual desire was by definition heterosexual; thus homosexual desire was the result of "mistaken" gender identification. Butches were the recognized lesbians, the true "inverts," and they were punished severely for their violation of gender norms.

In response, lesbians who desired mainstream acceptance needed to argue that they were indeed "real women," like their heterosexual sisters in most ways other than sexual preference. Making a convincing case required muting butch self-presentation. This was not necessarily a regressive position, or one to be easily dismissed. Upwardly mobile lesbians were trying to "diminish the stigma associated with lesbians, and integrate themselves into mainstream society" and "to have good jobs while never giving up their social life as lesbians" (137). Kennedy and Davis contrast these women with those who separated themselves entirely from lesbian communities and socialized only with a few friends. The first group participated actively in community life, even if in an oppositional way; they identified as people with a stake in the success or failure of their community.

The command to be discreet arose persistently around political action. When homophile activists picketed the White House and the Civil Service building in 1965 to protest policies that banned employment of homosexuals, firm rules on dress were followed. The guidelines for the action stated that dress and appearance will be "conservative and conventional." Women uniformly wore dresses, while men wore business suits, white shirts, and ties. This dress was also recommended for public meetings of organizations whenever heterosexuals might be present. Thus again "discretion" was coded in terms of middle-class norms of dress and comportment; "conservative and conventional" defined these particular outfits only for certain groups.

Contemporary lesbian and lesbigay politics demonstrate how little the politics of representation has changed. Today the periodicals are glossy, with mass middle-class circulation (although still delivered in opaque covers), but the debates they encompass and elide are virtually identical to their mimeographed ancestors. To illustrate the costs of such a strategy I will focus on the largest U.S. lesbian and gay political organization, the Human Rights Campaign, since the arrival of Elizabeth Birch as executive director in January 1995. Since its beginnings as the Human Rights Campaign Fund in the 1980s, the HRC has grown to an organization of 175,000 members. Focusing on legislative and electoral politics, the HRC lobbies members of Congress on issues related to gays and lesbians, encourages voting by lesbians and gays, and is creating grass-roots formations able to mobilize gays and lesbians at the state and local level throughout the United States. Their membership, agenda, and strategies are resolutely white, middle-class, and assimilationist. Unlike the National Gay and Lesbian Task Force, created in the 1970s, HRC engages in a narrowly focused politics of rights.

HRC's agenda coalesces with their presentation of a mythic public face of lesbianism, a face that is hard for many lesbians to recognize. As it does to people of color and working-class and poor queers, this public face isolates and hides butch lesbians. In so doing, it abandons opportunities for examination of the role of gender in homophobia as well as class divisions among lesbians. HRC's attempts to foster mainstream acceptance have put it in the same binds faced by homophile organizations of the 1950s and 1960s, and it has dramatically failed to expand the options for butch lesbians. Rather, HRC's participation in fostering assimilationist images further consolidates the isolation and abandonment of a core constituency of lesbians.

Elizabeth Birch, a former corporate litigator, opened her tenure at the HRC with a glossy newsletter featuring a picture of her taken in front of the U.S. Capitol. In the photograph, Birch is neatly coifed, with earrings and muted red lipstick. Inside, another picture taken from below shows her with legs and arms crossed, showing a bit of leg below her neat black dress. She reads as perky and competent. Is she lesbian? Without contextual framing, it is not clear. Her words, rather than her image, reveal her as lesbian.

Birch's ability to pass does not make her femme. As Joan Nestle (1992) has noted, many femmes are taken for heterosexual by lesbians as well as straights. Yet femmes are dressing for themselves and for other women;

they are part of an "erotic conversation between two women" rather than an attempt to pass. In contrast to a femme aesthetic, Birch's self-presentation participates in the corporate aesthetic of capitalist societies. In order to be corporate leaders, women must sacrifice hints of sexuality that might make them prey to male co-workers. Nonetheless, they are forced to retain gender. Corporate female gender is a matter of demonstrating that one is not a man while simultaneously minimizing the disastrous impact of this fact on the collective life of the corporation—in effect, disincorporating oneself from one's female body. Because female gender, however, is defined largely through sexuality, corporate women cannot hope to escape (hetero)sexuality entirely. Rather, they offer the most muted signifiers available: lipstick, but not too bright; skirts, but not too sexy; earrings, but no dangles. Such strategies reflect the continuing fear and rejection of "different" bodies within modern democracies. The corporate body, like the citizen body, remains a white male heterosexual one.

As a fashion statement, corporate femininity is one among many proliferating styles that occupy the contemporary social landscape. We need not worry simply because Birch herself dresses in a manner that inserts her comfortably into the corridors of power. Instead, we should put her dress in the context of HRC's aims and the variety of presentations it offers. Birch's self-presentation should be read not simply as hers alone, but as that of the HRC board, who selected her as executive director; or rather, the board chose Birch because she embodies the qualities they desire to convey. It is imperative, therefore, that we inquire into the stakes for the progress of a movement of empowerment in difference when its leaders make themselves indistinguishable from the mass of privileged white heterosexuals. Rather than ask whether Birch is hiding her lesbianism in order to be a successful public actor, we should ask other questions: given that Birch's career is that of the "professional lesbian," as it were, we might ask how she, and those who endorse and finance her, are presenting lesbianism and gayness. We can and should examine what sort of politics Birch and the HRC are engaged in. We cannot infer from Birch's clothes alone that the HRC's goals are assimilationist (though we can take a hint), but we can ask about who the organization works with and through, and what can be accomplished through those venues. In short, how does the HRC introduce lesbianism into public discourse and politics?

The HRC, like virtually all proponents of the new gay discourse, is very firm in its position that homosexuality is a sexual orientation that is fixed from birth or very early childhood. This orientation is publicly relevant only insofar as others oppress us on that basis. The new gay visibility relies on what Cook and Hartnett (1999) in their study of the media portrayal of lesbians and gays, labeled "essentialist individualism." In this schema, "sexual orientation is not a choice, and we should judge these persons as individuals in many ways just like 'us,' the heterosexual reporter and audience" (17). This message explicitly appeals to heterosexuals to tolerate sexual minorities because (a) they can't help it; (b) sexuality is innate, so your kids aren't at risk of being recruited; and (c) they are really like us in most ways. This message gains credibility, both in mainstream news and in writing by sexual minorities, when its proponents condemn aspects of life that are not readily assimilable; most of us, they say, are decent.

Ultimately, the HRC deflects questions of sexual behavior in favor of presenting homosexuality as a mere status difference. Its picture of homosexuality is one of a private and innocuous difference. What matters in public is not what we do "in bed," but our merit as hard-working patriotic citizens and our desire to live a life centered on family, work, and community. This presentation is in accord with the HRC's political goals. The HRC seeks non-discrimination laws in housing, credit, and employment; an end to the de facto military ban of queers; and same-sex marriage. It is, in fact, the quintessentially liberal agenda. Rather than suggesting, as Teresa de Lauretis (1991, iii) puts it, that "contemporary queer sexualities may be reconceptualized as social and cultural forms in their own right," the HRC presents homosexuality as simply a category to be re-relegated to the private sphere precisely through political action to combat discrimination. In the absence of discrimination, they seem to imply, homosexuals will fit right in to capitalist America.

As we enter the public world through the Human Rights Campaign, we are urged to leave our desiring bodies at home. Our differences as lesbian or gay people become nothing more than a question of whom we go home to. Like the assimilationist Jew, whose only difference is where and when s/he worships, this homosexual's difference offers no apparent challenge to existing social structures. And just as such Jews must constantly check themselves to guard against seeming "too Jewish," the HRC seems to ward off queerness even as it invokes gay and lesbian identities. In its lobbying activity, as in its literature, the HRC eschews queerness for a focused media-ready campaign. Although some of the group's national media celebrities may be read as butch, by and large HRC spokespeople present bland all-American images.

Candace Gingrich, sister of Newt Gingrich, provides a provocative example of the dialectic between intraminority and assimilationist sensibilities. Gingrich was recruited as a spokesperson because of the embarrassment she offered her brother. She is the most visibly butch of the HRC celebrities, and the most clearly working-class. The photos in her book are a testament to image management: while the captions beneath home pictures stress her gender non-conformity, the cover photograph includes both a slightly longer hair cut and lipstick (Gingrich 1996). One suspects that HRC managers did not read the captions to the photos.

Assimilation and Invisibility

Although it is safe to assume that the primary audience of the HRC report is gay (and, to a lesser extent, lesbian), Birch's self-presentation seems aimed not at these groups but at the always-watching heterosexual population; or rather, it is aimed at those gays and lesbians who identify themselves with their heterosexual neighbors and families, who want to minimize their difference—the "silent majority" of virtually normal strangers. Those who cherish their difference, who value their forms of desire, sensibility, and expression not for how they resemble heterosexual forms but in their own right, have no place in the HRC universe.

Such exclusion may seem to many to be dictated by the concerns of practical politics, but it is not only strategic; rather, it presents the image of gays and lesbians that many, perhaps most, American gays and lesbians seek to realize in their lives. It is nonetheless a shortsighted practice. The "de-gaying" of HRC collaborates in the deeper homophobia that motivates resistance to equal rights. The homosexuality that is enacted in these legislative arenas is a sexuality only of discourse, a sexuality mentioned but never revealed. Failing to address or acknowledge the extent of anti-gay sentiment that runs throughout the United States, the HRC nonetheless reacts to that sentiment by divesting itself of the traces of (homo)sexual difference. In effect, the HRC's policy is to "tell," to violate the military's rule, but only through avowals and never through acts. Such visible gay-rights leaders present themselves in a manner calculated to make their difference invisible except as a matter of abstract words.[3] This effort is not unique to HRC, or to gay-rights activism. As Joshua Gamson (1996) describes, for civil-rights activists, "at least the appearance of normality is central to gaining political 'room.' Rights are gained, according to this logic, by demonstrating similarity (to heterosexual people, to other minority groups) in a non-threatening manner" (402). I do not want to reject the imperative of finding bases for affiliation and sympathy, nor do I wish to deny the importance of civil rights, but I do want to caution against the belief that such strategies and goals are sufficient for social transformation. Even those who truly desire nothing more than the right to hold down an executive position and buy a luxury condo with their spouse will be ill served by detaching legal struggles from cultural visibility.

Butch lesbians are caught by the strictures of a movement that demands respectability as the price of inclusion and equality. Respectability is not simply a matter of treating oneself and others with respect and integrity. It requires careful attention and obedience to prevailing norms of dress and comportment. Unfortunately for butches, it is precisely their deviation from these norms that marks them as visible lesbians. A movement that demands assimilation as the price of equality fails to fully grasp the oppression of lesbians, an oppression that is rooted in gender norms as much as in proscriptions on sexuality. The failure of mainstream movement leaders to grasp this point is a result of the privileging of (homo)sexuality as an independent axis of oppression distinct from gender. This isolation has been recurrent throughout male gay movement history. In the 1950s and 1960s, most male homophile activists called on lesbians to work with them against anti-gay prejudice. Often, however, this work amounted to the women making coffee and taking notes. With the rise of feminism lesbians developed an effective language for resisting male privilege, but the men remained largely unaware of the problem. Recent activism, both mainstream and queer, has been quite effective at mobilizing a broad range of people who earlier had remained closeted or did not introduce sexuality into their politics. However, this new wave of activism has reintroduced the problem of gender.

Mainstream erasure operates through the production of images that recode lesbianism for a mass audience nervous about what equality for homosexuals might mean. This erasure is visible in the best efforts of mainstream media to present sympathetic treatments, such as the 1992 *Newsweek* cover story featuring a photo of a lesbian couple. This photo showed a white couple, well-scrubbed, both with "normal" haircuts. One could be read as slightly more butch than the other, but neither violated visual codes of the girl next door. It was, of course, possible to read the photo through lesbian lenses. These women were not like lesbians consumed in male porn, long-haired Playboy bunnies fondling one another. They were believable as lesbians to lesbians—but just barely. The accompanying article followed their lives and those of other gays and lesbians without hinting that one was the "man," as earlier treatments might have. It was, in fact, a model of the new gay marketing strategy. It was also profoundly disappointing to many lesbians of my acquaintance, as it seemed to leave us out in the same old sexual Siberia. Where were the lesbians who looked like us, either butch/femme couples or unreconstructed lesbian-feminists? Where were the lesbians who look like dykes? *Newsweek's* liberal desire to demonstrate that we're just like other girls served to bolster support for those lesbians who *are* just like other girls. The rest of us, it seems, are still out of luck.

The presentation of a respectable lesbian population, because it avoids the subconscious aversion and fear of heterosexuals, can only go so far in fostering equality. Those who argue that we should "show our best face" demonstrate their inadequate understanding of the stakes of the battle. First, their standards of a "good" face are as resolutely middle-class as those of the earlier homophile movement. What face looks best depends upon the cultural norms of a given population. Defining as the "best face" that which accords with white middle-class heterosexual norms amounts to abandoning any claims for autonomy or alternative aesthetics. Second, such arguments suggest that butchness is an optional presentation, an "affectation" as Sullivan would have it. This argument implies that lesbians are all "really" women, so it won't hurt if we dress and act like them at certain moments. Mainstream gay organizations and writers treat butchness as drag, failing to recognize and honor butch experience and identities as valuable modes of life that are neither simply inherent nor merely performance, but complex and stubborn clusters of perception, desire, and subjectivity. If "participation means being able to speak in one's own voice, and thereby simultaneously to construct and express one's cultural identity through idiom and style" (Fraser 1992, 126), the new gay visibility both opens and forecloses participation. The path that leads to inclusion through the sacrifice (or privatization) of gender non-conformity and distinctive sensibilities limits not only those obvious rebels but that within everyone that might be a little too queer for comfort.

As an example of a contrasting possibility, the National Lesbian and Gay Task Force's choice in 1994 of Melinda Paras as executive director demonstrated what the end of homophobia might really mean. Paras's public presentation confronts and challenges stereotypes of lesbians not by disproving them, but by combining visible gender non-conformity with political and personal efficacy. Her confidence with a butch presentation is perhaps not coincidentally linked to a leftist politics, and her appointment reflects the more grass-roots leftist history of NGLTF. Historically, NGLTF has had a broader agenda than that of newer organizations such as HRC. It has been less wedded to respectability, as it has been a broader-based community-building organization as well as a legislative force. The fact that Paras is also a woman of color (as is Urvashi Vaid, her predecessor as executive director) also speaks to NGLTF's broader vision and willingness to provide a public face at odds with dominant norms. Although racism and sexism still exist within NGLTF (Vaid 1995), the visibility of butch women in the organization reflects a broader vision of change as well as a different conception of who can represent "our" issues.

As the United States moves toward a so-called service economy, and as labor positions move overseas, self-presentation becomes more central to the lives of Americans. Those who do not "look right" may find themselves without jobs, or in the bottom tier of income. Organizations that concern themselves with the welfare of lesbians must link formal rights to larger economic questions if they are to make a real difference in the lives of butch lesbians. An equality that does not include an end to butch-bashing and stigmatization is a "virtual equality" (Vaid 1995), an equality for those who fit the parameters of disembodied "rational persons." A liberal agenda does nothing to change the attitudes of those of all sexualities who fear and hate gender non-conformity. Activism that insists on respectability and polices its own members in the name of acceptability has already betrayed those it claims to represent. In order to fulfill the goals of queer equality and empowerment, lesbian and gay organizations need to consciously choose to support and be proud of all members of their communities. The "good" perverts cannot buy rights by distancing themselves from the "bad" ones. Not only is it a betrayal of those who bear the most extreme brunt of violence and hatred, it is short-sighted because the powerful forces arrayed against equality will continue to rely on fears of gender disorder to threaten any gains that are made. The challenge for gay and lesbian politics is not to sanitize or arrange us; it is to provide spaces in which people may or may not be out, may or may not be visible, to foster plural worlds and spheres. This must be both our strategy and our goal.

The Queer Response

The new gay visibility affords the most widely disseminated images and discussions by sexual minorities in the United States. It is not, however, the only avenue of such images and discussions. Aside from the presentations of the New Right (see Herman 1997), another response to strangeness emerged in the 1990s. For a younger generation of activists, the post-post-Stonewall generation, "lesbian and gay" is the name of stodgy, respectable men and women who happen to like sex with other men and women, and who want in on the dominant centers of power. "Lesbian and gay" is the constituency of the HRC or the Victory Fund; it is writers such as Bawer and Sullivan. (In this conception, lesbians are largely invisible except under the sign of feminism, the ogre of sexual restriction and moralization.) Thus, "queer" is to the current generation as "gay" was to the 1970s, a mark of pride, a throwing off of closets and politeness, and a bid for autonomous culture. Reprising their elders, younger queer activists seek neither separatism nor assimilation, but the reshaping of the public and private spheres so as to give presence and meaning to non-heterosexual desires.

The rejection of "gay and lesbian" as the sign of an outmoded respectability is perhaps most evident in "queerzines," self-published guerilla productions. Zines create alternative media by publishing readers' letters and articles on a par with the editors' work, encouraging participation by those who cannot afford or do not want the glossy new magazines. They are vociferously anti-respectability and identify "gay and lesbian" with the quest for respectability: *BIMBOX*, one of the most visible zines, announced itself a "gay and lesbian-free zone," "at war with lesbians and gays" (Barnard 1996, 75). And why the war? Johnny Noxzema, one of the editors of *BIMBOX*, wrote to the *Advocate*, the most prominent gay and lesbian national magazine, to explain: "[Y]our generation of misogynist capitalist swine clones and half-baked numbskull granola feminists over 30 are directly responsible for . . . segregated bars, sexism, racism, classism, separatism, mass complacency, and a complex network of selfish, over-educated, self-appointed rich people overseeing a vast fake-democratic lesbian and gay multinational bureaucracy that dictates how we think, dress, act, and fuck" (ibid.).

But "queer" is not just a generational renaming of a stable periodic occurrence. Queer politics is more complex than the politics of gay visibility. Not only does queer politics explicitly disavow assimilation, it is less organized and representable than gay and lesbian politics. Queer politics largely absents itself from legislative politics, finding a base in academic and urban cultural centers instead. This absence does not imply a lesser concern with citizenship; "queer citizenship" has been the subject of numerous articles, books, and dissertations over the past five years (e.g., Berlant 1997; Dunlap and Jones 1996). Themes of citizenship and publicity are just as prominent in queer writing and activism as they are in the new gay discourse, but they are played in quite different keys for different audiences.

Queer politics is also more difficult to characterize than lesbian and gay politics because of the notable variety of uses and implications of the term "queer." While "gay" and "lesbian" have widely agreed-upon (though by no means unproblematic) meanings, seeming to function as simple substitutes for "homosexual," "queer" both is and is not the name of a particular sexuality. Queer points to non-normative sexualities, but also suggests a political valence and understanding of those sexualities. It is, thus, again rather like "gay" in 1970. In the 1970s gay liberation was the name of a major theoretical challenge to assimilation as well as minoritization. Early activists and writers argued that gay liberation could transform all sexual and gender relations; they argued against marriage and monogamy and against existing family structures

(Altman 1981; Jay and Young 1972). Indeed, as Gary Lehring (1997) notes, their views are altogether too radical and anti-essentialist for many contemporary students who identify as queer). I am consequently using the labels "queer" and "gay" not to signal clear differences between camps, but widespread perceptions and self-perceptions of such differences.

The major disagreement that queers have with gays concerns assimilation. The quotes from *BIMBOX* suggest that assimilation is inherently undesirable, not only because of the price paid in order to fit in but because the dominant order is inherently unethical and undesirable. Other major public queer documents of the 1990s, such as the "I Hate Straights" flyer passed out at many pride marches in the early 1990s, reject assimilation not as undesirable (though that runs through these pieces as well) but as impossible (Blasius and Phelan 1997). Straights hate queers, "I Hate Straights" tells us, and hating them is simply a reasonable response to being hated. The dream of reconciliation and acknowledgment is just that, an empty dream. Attempts to assimilate are thus indicted both for their acceptance of the worst features of contemporary American life and for their futility.

Queers may thus seem united in their disdain for assimilation, but this impression is mistaken. What exactly is non-assimilation and the political position that it entails? One young queer put it thus: "Queer implies to me, new and non-establishment and different, non-assimilationist. They want to work from within and I just want to crash in from the outside and say 'Hey! Hello, I'm queer. I can make out with my girlfriend. Ha Ha. Live with it. Deal with it. Out of my way.' . . . [T]he gay and lesbian movement, the queer movement, the dyke movement is about doing what feels right to you without catching any flak ever" (Bond 1991, 18). To the extent that this statement is representative of queers, it poses a major concern for queer politics. Here anti-assimilationism slides into liberal individualism; rather than offering an articulation of social justice, the speaker demands a world without judgment, without contest, without politics. And this has indeed been one representative strain of queer activism and thinking. Fearing the labels of moralism or tradition, some queers refuse any appeals to standards of conduct as impositions. They are, of course, not alone in this; many liberationist movements and rhetorics develop in this direction. But in the long run, such refusals run

the risk of limiting their impact on the culture(s) they contest by refusing to engage. Rebellion is not necessarily social change. The danger of
anti-assimilation politics is precisely that of confusing rebellion with
transformation. Ignoring the neighbors, or deliberating inflaming them,
is not a revolutionary act, but liberalism's focus on the individual as the
only social actor makes it hard for Americans to find their way past this
point.

Sue Dunlap and Kathleen Jones (1996) provide a poignant example
of the limitations of defiance as a social strategy. Writing about the 1996
Republican National Convention in San Diego, they contrast the strategies of Gay and Lesbian Families of America to present "positive"
images on billboards and bus shelters, and VOICES '96, which argued
for confrontation of "family values" rather than endorsement. (Inter-
estingly, VOICES '96 was supported by virtually every state, local, and
national organization.) VOICES '96 articulated a democratic, public
"queer" set of values and goals, but its action was confined to protest-
ing within the allotted area for protests, an area easily avoidable by del-
egates. The billboard and bus campaign, while "conformist," was much
more visible and hard to contain. Which was the queer strategy?

For many, of course, queer thought and action cannot be contained
in such a simple formula. In their more organized and reflective forms,
queer theory and politics work both to valorize lesbian and gay sexualities and to challenge the categories and social structures within which
these sexualities have been formed. Rather than seeking legitimation
from heterosexual society, queers aim at conscious celebration of
homosexuality and rigorous examination of the strictures of gender,
race, and sexuality that produce its subordination.

This position is clearly articulated by Teresa de Lauretis, who
described the "speculative premise" of the first "queer theory" conference in 1990 as the idea

that homosexuality is no longer to be seen simply as marginal with regard to
a dominant, stable form of sexuality (heterosexuality) against which it would
be defined either by opposition or homology. In other words, it is no longer
to be seen either as merely transgressive or deviant vis-à-vis proper, natural
sexuality (i.e., institutionalized reproductive sexuality), according to the
older, pathological model, or as just another, optional 'life-style,' according to
the model of contemporary North American pluralism. Instead, male and
female homosexualities—in their current sexual-political articulations of gay

and lesbian sexualities, in North America—may be reconceptualized as social and cultural forms in their own right, albeit emergent ones and thus still fuzzily defined, undercoded, or discursively dependent on more established forms. (1991, iii)

Thus, for de Lauretis lesbian and gay sexualities are "forms of resistance to cultural homogenization, counteracting dominant discourses with other constructions of the subject in culture." Queer theory and politics aim at disruption of the dominant social text not via separatism, but through "demanding political representation while insisting on . . . material and historical specificity" (ibid).

In her formulation, de Lauretis largely equates "queer" with "lesbian and gay." This is indeed one major contemporary use of the term. This usage does not problematize membership in queerness, but signals a more utopian and confrontational stance than that associated with "lesbian and gay." De Lauretis's use of queer offers the possibility, but does not in itself effect, the destabilization of categories of gender and sexuality that is also central to queer theory. As we will see in the next chapter, this has presented problems for alliances with other sexual minorities. Even among gays and lesbians, however, claims to social and cultural distinctness are liable to be problematic.

The alternative to assimilation is to stake out space, geographical or cultural, in which to build an autonomous culture. Certainly this has been done to an amazing extent in San Francisco, Los Angeles, and New York, and to a lesser extent in Chicago, Boston, Atlanta, and other large cities. It is also fostered by print and electronic media that "bring queerness to one's door" (often still in plain envelopes). It is nonetheless a partial autonomy at best. For those outside large urban centers, no such culture exists. This does not mean that sexual minorities in these places are invisible, or that each individual is isolated; it simply means that there are too few to build something that might aspire to the term "culture." A bookstore or a bar does not a culture make. Nor does a shared sensibility, or a shared awareness of oppression. Even in large cities, where one may live much of one's life surrounded by queer people, doing business and earning one's living with them, the idea of a "homosexual culture" is deeply problematic. Aside from its presumption of unity and homogeneity, such an idea suggests not only networks, not only a distinctive sensibility, but an ethical and ontological consensus. To the extent that such a consensus emerges, it is at least partially due to its pre-existence in the members' cultures of origins. This may be true of any sexual culture anywhere; it is certainly true of lesbian and gay communities in the United States, where the mainstream is so prized.

We might also question the bid for autonomous culture because its success would entail so many temptations endemic to Western modernity. Cultures make new boundaries to distinguish their members from outsiders, and modernity reifies these boundaries into sharp binaries of in/out, good/bad, rational/irrational. A desire for autonomous culture, like the modern mantra of "self-determination," always includes a willful forgetting of who will be excluded in the new formation (or under what terms they will be included). We might then conclude not only that assimilation is inevitable, but also that it is not the worst fate to befall strangers.

Is Assimilation Inevitable?

Debates between and among gays and queers continue to resound with the desires for autonomy and recognition. In modernity these are presented as twins: recognition as a member is premised on personal autonomy (especially in the sense of self-mastery), while the goal of recognition is the protection of one's ability to pursue one's own goals. That things are not always so neat is evident from the history of the last century. For strangers in particular, these twins appear rather as Scylla and Charybdis— steering for recognition endangers one's ability to be different, forcing one to forswear differences that interfere with the assimilating body, while claims to autonomy founder on the problem of delineating a space that is both distinct from the mainstream and deserving of its protection. The production of communities of strangers does not lessen this dilemma. Communities provide places for strangers to get their bearings and to live without their difference constantly before them, but they also highlight that difference and introduce debates about how to live as that marked being.

For sexual strangers, the drive to assimilation is inevitable. This does not mean that it is successful or will be in the future; as debates between queers and gays demonstrate, it is not clear what would count as success. Rather, I mean to say that the quest for assimilation is inherent for sexual minorities even as many try to resist. This is so for several reasons.

First, sexual strangers do not grow up "outside" the dominant culture in any simple sense. The mantras of self-recognition stories in the new gay books are meant to capture precisely the shock at finding that one is not at home in one's home. Heterosexual culture is not a foreign country to which we come, but is our native land. Rejection by that culture is not a matter of barred entry—we are already here. Rather it is a matter of expulsion and exile, an exile that is lived in the midst of the expellers. Although for some this leads to conscious rejection of their native culture, for many more it does not. Instead, assimilation is a matter of regaining as consciously different a membership that was once taken for granted. This conscious difference does not entail a challenge to any other prevailing cultural norms. It may lead to that, but there is no automatic theoretical or practical linkage between social difference and rejection of social norms. The current "gayby boom" and "deurbanization" of homosexuality provide evidence that many if not most sexual strangers seek nothing more than to be at home in their communities of origin (Signorile 1997).

At another level, however, assimilation might prove to be an inevitable failure. The fate of the stranger is to be never fully inside nor fully outside. Moves toward assimilation work by reducing major differences (that is, those differences seen as major by the dominant group) to "private" differences. Such was the attempt of German Jews; such is the current fate of American Jewry (Brettschneider 1996; Rubin 1995). As Marx pointed out, however, assimilation requires the dominant group to treat a significant difference as insignificant, thereby belying its importance in the lives of the minority. The "inclusion" of sexual minorities in a state that continues to define itself as heterosexual, white, and masculine will be at best an addendum waiting to be nullified.

These remarks are far from all that might be said about the dilemmas of assimilation. They might, however, function to suggest what a less disciplined, perhaps queer, public discourse would be. In keeping with Jean-François Lyotard's admonition that justice "does not consist merely in the observance of the rules" but also, or most important, in "working at the limits of what the rules permit, in order to invent

new moves, perhaps new rules and therefore new games" (Lyotard and
Thebaud 1985, 100), and his belief that the most basic injustice is the
silencing of others, queer public discourse must seek to foster diversity
and competing views, not in order to subsume them into a grand syn-
thesis, but in order to give voice to the irreducible multiplicity of queer
possibilities. Nor should we expect the result of such discourse to be a
benign pluralism. A public discourse will encounter and challenge
opponents. This is not the same as personal attack, a form of "politics"
at which queer communities excel; it is serious, engaged debate without the expectation of resolution.

Because assimilationists ask nothing more of the state than to be
included in its rituals and rights in spite of their difference, theirs is
always an unstable politics of hope and fear—hope that they might be
included, and fear that the tide will turn. Both hope and fear encourage
groups of strangers to police their own members in order to appear fit
for membership. This policing in turn lessens whatever cultural autonomy might have emerged in the past, as well as the potential that
strangers might transform the culture they seek to join. It is to this
policing, and its costs, that we now turn.

5

Strangers among "Us"
Secondary Marginalization
and "LGBT" Politics

The questions of assimilation and of group presentation bear not only on lesbians and gays, but on all those marked as sexual strangers. Claiming respectability for one group of strangers often proceeds by implicitly or explicitly contrasting that group to others, constructing relations of similarity between those seeking entry and their gatekeepers while simultaneously articulating that group as "normal" compared to other groups. This happens both within groups, as when "good homosexuals" make their bid for entry by condemning "bad queers," and among groups that many see as closely allied. Indeed, whether a collection of people is seen as a group or as several groups depends largely on the process of articulation of group identity and politics (Laclau and Mouffe 1985). Such articulation is an ongoing, dynamic part of the politics of sexual strangers.

In recent years, gay and lesbian activists have received pressure for greater recognition from bisexuals and transgendered people. Decrying their quite different modes and bases for exclusion, these groups have challenged lesbians and gays to broaden their understandings of their communities and their politics. In response, many groups and individuals now regularly refer to "LGBT" communities and politics. Partisans of "queer," on the other hand, often claim that queer offers greater inclusiveness to all these groups by calling into question the very identities initialed in LGBT.

115

Whether queer or LGBT, the casual observer might well conclude that the project of inclusion is well under way. This conclusion, however, would be mistaken.

In communities subject to advanced marginalization, the access and privilege of some is conditional on the secondary marginalization of "the most vulnerable and stigmatized in their communities" (Cohen 1999, 27). Although bisexuals and transgendered people are not the only stigmatized groups within lesbian and gay communities, I focus here on these groups as larger signs of what is lost in the process of sexual marginalization. I will argue that although real inclusion seems politically risky, the risk is worth taking. Such inclusion requires some fundamental changes in existing lesbian and gay communities. These changes amount to a queering of communities that have been in retreat from their own queerness.

The history of relations among the four groups initialed in LGBT is hardly that of a community, unless we use that term in the vaguest manner. Lesbians and gays have often come together for a variety of reasons, but they have just as often separated from one another. How and why they come together is a result of conceptions of identity and social standing within communities. These conceptions in turn have structured the reception of bisexuals and transgendered people. I will argue here that, rather than extending existing understandings of sexual orientation and gender to "include" bisexuals and transgendered people, lesbians and gays should use the understandings of bi and trans people to reexamine their assumptions about what it means to be lesbian or gay. They should do this not in order to eliminate meaningful differences among the groups, but in order to envision an ontology and a politics that actively confront the position of strangeness in modernity rather than running from it or reacting to it.

Rejection and Appropriation

Bisexuals and transgendered people appear as strangers within lesbian and gay communities in ways startlingly similar to how lesbians and gays appear in heteronormative society. Strangers threaten because of their ambiguity rather than simply their difference. They look like "us," but they aren't; or, they might be, but for this one (or more) difference(s), the importance of which is continually under negotiation. Unlike the strangeness of queers in general in mainstream societies, though, the position of these two groups is characterized by an ambivalent dynamic of rejection and appropriation. Most strangers are simply overlooked in or rejected from community or polity imaginaries. Because the current construction of lesbian and gay identities and histories has been so bound to these two groups, however, they cannot be rejected in any simple sense. Rather, the dual processes of rejection and appropriation signal the importance of these groups to the construction of lesbian and gay identities as well as continuing ambiguity about the relations between sex, gender, and sexuality.

Bisexuals are strangers in lesbian and gay communities because they sometimes seem to fit in, then at other times don't; or, perhaps more threatening, they embody the possibility of simultaneously fitting and not fitting. In communities defined by object choice, a desire that fluctuates must necessarily be problematic. Nonetheless, many bisexuals are appropriated for lesbian and gay history, rewritten as gay or lesbian, when it serves the purpose of proving that "we are everywhere." This historical appropriation is in sharp contrast with the invisibility of contemporary bisexuals in lesbian and gay scholarship and activism (or the invisibility of their bisexuality). This dual reception is not surprising. Ancestors have spoken, and can no longer speak back; contemporaries continually present their strangeness and its challenges.

Perhaps not surprisingly, transgendered people suffer a similar stigma. Like bisexuals, they are alternately disavowed and appropriated by lesbians and gays: if dead, they are hailed as ancestors or martyrs; if alive, they are vilified as embarrassments to the "normal" homosexuals. Contemporary homosexual politics has worked to separate gender from sexuality so as to enable homosexuals to claim normal manhood or womanhood. Transgendered people do not belong in this normal community. Gay bars that welcome transgendered embodiments continue to be those at the bottom of the homosexual social scale, in the worst neighborhoods, facing the greatest violence. For many normal homos, the presence of transgendered embodiment is the key element marking off certain bars as "low class" or pride parades as "over the top." Ki Namaste (1997, 185–89) has noted how drag queens and transsexuals are relegated to the status of "entertainment" in gay communities, not speakers on a podium or equal political participants but performers. In many communities, these "low-class" trans/drag bars have the strongest politics, best participation, and highest fundraising in the community—and in return they are ignored and hidden away.

This marginalization has recently shown signs of giving way to a broader politics. Since 1995, the Human Rights Campaign has increasingly reached out to transgendered people and has pledged to support an amendment to the proposed Employment Non-Discrimination Act (ENDA) that would add transgendered status as a protected category. In May 1999 the National Gay and Lesbian Task Force adopted the stronger position of pledging not to support ENDA unless "sexual expression" as well as "sexual orientation" is included. This comes partly in response to a survey that found that over a quarter of those lesbians, gays, and bisexuals who experienced job discrimination reported that the discrimination was due in part to their gender expression. The survey makes clear that the strangeness of sexual minorities is deeply bound to their perceived deviance from gender norms.

Nonetheless, neither the large organizations nor most of the new gay discourse questions the reification of "sexual orientation" as an issue distinct from that of transgender. The drive to assert the distinction between gender and sexual orientation is part of a larger campaign to establish the normality of lesbians and gays, a normality in which transgendered people do not share. Nor, for that matter, do bisexuals; because bisexuals challenge the idea of a fixed sexual orientation, the cultural metaphors of instability surrounding bisexuality make them less than desirable allies.

The exclusion of bisexuals and transgendered people from lesbian or gay communities and politics is thus a product of two forces. First, the push to assimilate into existing cultural and legal categories is facilitated by notions of sexual orientation as fixed and binary. If homosexuals are "born that way," their presence does not pose a challenge to the heterosexual identities and futures of others. This point has been prominent in legal arguments for equality as well as in media presentations (Currah 1996; Herman 1997). As Paisley Currah (1996, 58) has argued, "immutability arguments" "correspond not only to popular fictions about rights and immutability but also to the prevailing legal standards in US constitutional law." Legal standards for protection from discrimination, largely derived from the model of racial oppression, require that the group in question manifest "immutable characteristics" that make it a "discrete and insular minority." Thus, opponents of equality claim that homosexuality is chosen (although, as Herman notes, the argument over immutability is gradually receding within Christian Right discourse) (Herman 1997, 69–75, 120–25). Among the public, there is a correlation between acceptance of immutability and sympathy for equality (*New York Times* 5 March 1993, cited in Currah 1996, 82 n. 20).

The law, however, is not the only reason that gay and lesbian advocates have insisted on immutability. Although other minorities such as religious minorities are not required to show that they are immutable, life-long members of their sects, lesbian and gay activists have been reluctant to make the analogy between religion and sexuality. Because majorities of Americans continue to find homosexuality immoral, even as they endorse equal political and economic rights, activists have been reluctant to make arguments that might offend judges and the heterosexual majority. Further, many if not most American gays and lesbians now believe that sexual orientation is immutable, so they might be reluctant to adopt arguments that neglect what they see as a central element of their identity and their oppression.

The second element in the crafting of mainstream arguments is the assertion that gays and lesbians do not challenge prevailing gender structures. If they are, as many insist, just like heterosexuals in their gender conformity, then they are not a threat to existing conceptions of masculinity, femininity, or sexual difference. Andrew Sullivan's narrative of masculinity lost and found (1995), in which gender deviance is a product of the closet that is naturally left behind upon finding acceptance from heterosexuals, explicitly aligns him with "normal" men and against transgendered people. The Human Rights Campaign's closeting of butch lesbians and drag queens similarly reassures its constituencies that inclusion will require no reconsideration of gender.

As Joshua Gamson (1998) has shown, the stigmatization of bisexuals and transgendered people on talk shows, stigmatization in which lesbians and gay men participate, has been essential to the construction of homosexuality as normal. Gamson argues that "the moral defense of homosexuality, in fact, is shaped by the frequent dismissal of transgendered and bisexual people on TV talk. When same-sex desire is linked to nonmonogamy (as it so often is on programs dealing with bisexuality), or when it is closely associated with gender-crossing . . . we hit a brick wall in the drive toward a morality of love, freedom, and acceptance" (135). Nor, he notes, was this limit reached only by heterosexual viewers, audiences, or producers: gay and lesbian participants, whether "experts" or everyday people, solidify their normality on these shows by contrasting their stable, gender-conforming lives to these "others."

It is no coincidence, therefore, that the mainstream strategies of some gay and lesbian activists elide the existence of bisexuals and transgendered people. The absence of these groups is essential to the success of the two arguments upon which these activists base their claims for normality. The challenges that bisexuals and transgendered people bring to gay and lesbian politics are distinct, but they converge on the inability of gay and lesbian activists to come to grips with the position of strangers in heteronormative society. The exclusion of bisexual and transgendered people is not solely a result of political strategizing based on ideas about what heterosexuals will tolerate, but this factor is not absent: as Gamson notes, many argue that legal changes such as the Employment Non-Discrimination Act will not be achieved unless bisexuals and transgendered people are left out. But the major national organizations have largely changed their tune over the last five years. Rather than being a product of political calculation, the marginalization of these groups is intimately related to the quest for an identity on the part of lesbians and gays. The modern intolerance of ambivalence, what Zygmunt Bauman (1991) calls the "legislative" attitude of modernity in which apparent chaos is ordered through successive inside/outside distinctions, is not absent from gay and lesbian communities and individuals. Nor is it present only in those who might be called assimilationist; although organizations such as the Human Rights Campaign and writers such as Sullivan provide highly visible examples of such intolerance, it manifests in a wide range of abjections, abhorrences, and fears. Although they are not more biphobic or transphobic than heterosexuals, and many are less so, lesbian and gay communities participate in larger modern fears about ambivalence and boundary crossing. As participants in the modern "legislation" of and discourse about homosexuality, they have both challenged and accepted hegemonic ideas about gender, sexuality, race, and class. Ending the exclusion of bisexuals and transgendered people requires moving from liberal notions of tolerance to an understanding of and challenge to popular models of homosexuality as well as race, class, and gender. A short history is in order.

Paradigms and/of Exclusion

Modern treatments of homosexuality have operated through two main models. The first model considers homosexuality as sexual inversion. In this model, lesbians desire women because they are "really" men, or at least are more like men than are heterosexual women. Sexologists such as Richard von Krafft-Ebing and Havelock Ellis presented perhaps the clearest treatments of this model. Even Freud, who strenuously argued against conflating sexual object choice and physical or psychic gender in men, agreed that "real" lesbians are inevitably more masculine than non-lesbians. This heterosexualized model, for all its logical inconsistencies, remains the dominant understanding among heterosexuals, and among many gays and lesbians.

The second model focuses on the "homo" in homosexuality, the quest for the same, to suggest that lesbians are more womanly than heterosexuals, and gay men more manly than straight men, because they form bonds unadulterated by the other. This model is evident in early twentieth-century gay organizations such as the Committee of the Special in Germany and the Paris lesbian circle of Natalie Barney, and in contemporary lesbian-feminism. This homoerotic model essentializes masculinity and femininity while rejecting the ideology of complementarity that lies at the heart of modern heteronormativity.

The political consequences of these two models are quite different. The first model suggests that gays and lesbians are more alike than not, sharing a middle space on a gender continuum. Karl Ulrichs's nineteenth-century conception of a continuum from "real (heterosexual, masculine) men" to masculine gays to feminine gays to masculine lesbians and finally to "real women" exemplifies this thinking. Edward Carpenter's conception of homosexuals as a "third sex" popularized this understanding among gays and lesbians. Claiming Native American *berdaches* and Indian *hjiras* as ancestors, adherents to this conception claim commonality for gays and lesbians on the basis of their presumed gender inversion.

This idea of a common ground is easily reinforced by laws and other hegemonic practices that stigmatize homosexuality in both men and women. Thus "homosexuality" becomes the name for an axis of sociopolitical identification and action. That identification has been least problematic for gay white men, who have seen homosexuality as their distinguishing characteristic. For this group, all homosexuals have a common oppression and a common goal. Issues of gender, racial, or class inequality take a back seat to this presumed common interest.

The politics of the second model is perhaps the opposite of this. For the homoerotic man, homosexuality provides a shared masculine bond and way of life. Drawing on ancient Greece as a model, writers in this vein have celebrated the manliness of men together (Blasius and Phelan 1997, 152–69). Lesbian-feminists likewise have argued that they have little in common with gay men, as gay men's sexual practices and culture are quite different from lesbian mores and often involve dismissal and exclusion of women (Blasius and Phelan 1997, 498–521).

We thus have two models of what homosexual desire involves and implies. Neither has been at all satisfactory. As totalities, they have largely colluded in dominant ideas about gender. The idea that loving women is evidence of masculinity is not only heterosexist, it is contradicted by daily evidence. However, loving women is also not evidence of one's greater womanliness. If lesbian desire is not necessarily masculine desire, neither is it clearly feminine or feminist. As the writing and activism of bi and trans people makes clear, and as I will explain more later, we are not just one sex or one gender, nor are those we desire.

Both of these models fail insofar as they fail to problematize the categories of woman and man. By assuming that all "women" are the same in some key way, a way that is usually left undefined, they occlude the variety of ways of being a woman, as well as the myriad identifications and gaps of identification that are experienced by those who claim or are assigned the status of woman. These assumptions are illuminated at certain moments, most conspicuously when transgendered people's inclusion is at stake. The exclusion of male-to-female (MTF) trans people from "women's" events has initiated important discussions about the status of woman as a category. More recent controversy over female-to-male (FTM) trans people incites different, though related, problems with our categories of gender.

Exclusion is not simply a matter of residual marginalization, however. As Kathleen Chapman and Michael du Plessis (1997) have recently argued, attacks on and exclusion of transgendered people have played an integral role in securing a binary sex/gender system within feminism: "the use of transgender issues, concerns, subjectivities, and representations as markers of the limits against which feminist and lesbian selves and communities are defined" is part of a larger project to secure the identity of "woman" in a potentially chaotic environment (170). Rather than following from a prior construction of woman, transgendered people are crucial others for the construction of women in such lesbian-feminist discourse. That this is the case is demonstrated perhaps most clearly by the reception of Janice Raymond's anti-trans *The Transsexual Empire*. This book, published in 1979 and reissued in 1994, became a central text in lesbian-feminist theorizing about "woman" long before a visible and effective trans community developed. Sheila Jeffreys's *The Lesbian Heresy* (1993) and her more recent work have continued this theme, arguing that transsexuality and transgender are antifeminist—for MTF transsexuals because they appropriate women's space and "pretend" to be women, for FTM transsexuals because they abandon women for manhood. For both Jeffreys and Raymond, the social construction of gender and sexuality reaches its limits at the body.

Lesbian-feminists are not, of course, alone in this use of transgender to consolidate their identities. Modern gay politics since Freud has insisted on the distinction between sexual object choice and gender identity, and gay politics has implicitly contrasted the otherwise "normal" homosexual to the "gender dysphoric" transsexual. The diagnosis of gender dysphoria in the Diagnostic and Statistical Manual followed the removal of homosexuality as a pathology, and its continued pathologization has not been an object of discussion in gay or lesbian communities except insofar as gender dysphoria has been coded as gay (Sedgwick 1993, 154–64). Most public gay discourse continues to treat gender nonconformity as a lie spread by anti-gay forces, a slur on respectable men and women. The healthy homo has been constructed throughout the twentieth century, whether in Freud, homophile discourse, gay liberation (with some significant exceptions), or current public discourse, by explicit contrast with and renunciation of the sick gender nonconformist.

If the treatment of transgendered people illuminates the extent to which lesbians and gays remain attached to traditional gender categories, the reception of bisexuals offers insight into the continued commitment to ideas of a fixed sexual orientation. Bisexuals continue to be presented in public under the sign of promiscuity and all the evils believed to follow from it, most notably sexually transmitted diseases, especially AIDS. More fundamentally threatening, however, is the way that bisexuals disrupt the dichotomy between immutability and choice, not because all bisexuals deny that they were "born bisexual" (many insist that they were, and some argue that all humans are innately bisexual), but because their "orientation" crosses the lines of gender that immutability holds inviolate. If one can be attracted to either men or women, the lines that separate or link gender and desire cannot be stabilized. This becomes a direct sexual threat to heterosexuals: having been promised that lesbians are born, not made, seems to promise safety for heterosexual women. Even if a lesbian is attracted to a heterosexual woman, that woman may rest comfortably with the defense that she can't change any more than the lesbian can. But if bisexuality is a possibility, current heterosexuals might have to consider whether a flirtation might not change them in ways that they find distressing.

Bisexuality also confounds the model of homosexuality as gender inversion: If gay men are "like women," are bi men between hetero and gay men? The recent study that found that lesbians' inner ears are more like men's than the ears of heterosexual women left open the question of bisexuals. They were said to be "in between"—but in between what? Lesbians and straight women, or dykes and men? How neat the world would be if we could mark off territories in this way, as scientists hope to do. In fact, the dominant gendered discourse about homosexuality largely leaves bisexuality invisible, as it assumes that we all "are" one way or another.

In contrast to mainstream ideas of "in-betweenness," the position of bisexuals in lesbian communities has been developed through the homoerotic model of sexual orientation, extended to a homosolidaristic political community. If lesbians are most womanly, and most feminist, then bisexuals are less womanly and less feminist than lesbians (Rust 1995). Tainted by their association with men, bisexual women endanger the otherwise pure community. Insufficiently "inverted," bisexuals are also seen as politically unreliable. Both the inversion model and the theory of homoeroticism thus place bisexuality in a troubled and troubling position. If the homoerotic model presents bisexuals as unreliable allies, the inversion model participates in the assumption that everyone is either straight or gay. Thus, bisexuals are either gays who won't or can't admit that fact, or they are sexual tourists. Stereotyped as immature, unstable, unwilling to commit, untrustworthy, bisexual people are demonized in both dominant and lesbian and gay discourses.

Too Queer? Queer Enough?

Both trans and bi people have fought these exclusions. Their fights are not identical by any means. Bisexuals debate between the need to form their own communities and the desire to be included in lesbian and gay ones. Trans discussions are more ambivalent about inclusion, focusing more on constructing gender communities that cross lines of sexuality. Both groups have, however, an important political and conceptual relation to lesbian and gay communities. In response, many locations and communities have witnessed a sea change in the 1990s. Following the loss of hegemony of lesbian-feminism and the ascendancy of "queer," many lesbians and gays have tried to be inclusive. The label LGBT is an example of this new inclusiveness. A coalitional label, LGBT asserts a common goal. In conjunction with the term "community," LGBT suggests spaces where these four groups live and work together and create new meanings. This is an important shift from previous regimes of principled, explicit rejection and exclusion.

So far, however, I am not convinced by LGBT. As an inclusive label, LGBT enables lesbians and gays to deny charges of exclusion without actually changing their understandings or their lives. B and T are not only at the end of the line of initials; they remain the conceptual and political periphery of L and G communities.

This marginalization is present in queer theory as well as in political practice. Jay Prosser (1998, 14) has recently noted the ways in which transsexuals have been treated both as "literalizing the body" and therefore supporting gender systems, and as "deliteralizing" and subverting the assumed link between sex and gender. Transsexuals therefore become both not queer enough and the prototype of queer. The collapse of trans into queer, Prosser argues, serves queer more than it does trans subjects: inclusion becomes "the mechanism by which queer can sustain its very queerness—prolong the queerness of the moment—by periodically adding subjects who appear ever queerer precisely by virtue of their marginality in relation to queer" (58). With a theoretical investment that is perhaps the opposite of political efforts at normalization and inclusion, queer theory nonetheless appropriates trans subjects without acknowledging their perspectives.

The treatment of bisexuality in queer theory is equally fraught with difficulty, though of a different kind. Bisexuality, it seems, is not quite queer enough for queer theory. Judith Butler's entire treatment of bisexuality in *Gender Trouble* (1990) consists of a repudiation of the idea of an original, prediscursive bisexual disposition. Butler's description of heterosexual melancholia and her failure (refusal?) to account for homosexuality in psychoanalytic terms leave readers with a binary between heterosexual and queer (for which homosexuality is the privileged term) that once again leaves us to wonder whether bisexuality as an adult subject position can be anything other than "in between" or "some of each." Are bisexuals sort of melancholic? What is the dynamic of loss and introjection for bisexuals? Butler does not elaborate. Nor, for that matter, does Eve Sedgwick (indeed, bisexuality does not appear in the indexes to *Epistemology of the Closet* [1990] or *Tendencies* [1993], two volumes extensively concerned with binaries).

The difficulty with bisexuality in these texts is not due to any limitations on the part of their authors. Bisexuality consistently falls outside of both the medical model and the homoerotic one, thus confounding analyses that implicitly rely on either. Behind most recent queer theorizing, for all its valorization of agency, lies the continued belief that homosexuals just are that way, that to question how they appeared is to participate in homophobia. Likewise, bisexuality appears to be of interest only as an anomalous failure to "be all you can be." The homoerotic model, on the other hand, treats heterosexuality as interesting only to the extent that it is a cover for homoerotic bonding or an engagement of convenience (as Shakespeare would have it, the earth must be peopled). Thus, while transgender may be both not queer enough and too queer, within either prevailing model bisexuality is just not queer enough.

Oscillating Agency

The marginalization of bisexuality and transgender produces a loss not only for those "in" those categories, but for everyone. Bisexuality and transgender are the phenomena operating most strongly today to challenge and transform ideas about gender and sexuality. The promise of bisexuality and transgender lies precisely in the string of words used as epithets—unstable, uncommitted, fence-sitters—as well as in the inescapability of agency they both entail. These are insults to those who remain convinced that salvation and inclusion must come from establishing a clear identity and fighting for its inclusion. To these people instability is an insult and a threat. If our sexuality defines a line of battle, then being uncommitted becomes proof of unreliability. If, however, we understand the stakes of sexual politics in more universal terms, we see that the questions of mobility and choice are exactly the ones we must focus on.

Elizabeth Daumer (1992, 98) has argued that the perspective of bisexuality offers the chance to illuminate "the gaps and contradictions of all identity" and "the at times radical discontinuities between an individual's sexual acts and affectional choices, on the one hand, and her or his affirmed political identity, on the other." Daumer argues that destabilizing identity moves us toward a more progressive politics for several reasons. First, awareness of identity's incompleteness fosters appreciation for diversity both within and between individuals. Second, disarticulating identity, sexual act, and desire forces us to find a political ground for alliances, a vision for the future rather than a simple claim of identity. Without disavowing identity politics, we are led to incorporate our identities into a politics of ideas (Highleyman 1995). Our political dreams cannot rest with our own affirmation and comfort, because we might change our identities and desires. We need to build a politics that allows for shifts even as we affirm present identities.

What are the vision and the center of this politics? Most fundamentally, they are choice and agency. The threat of bisexuality has always been choice. Bisexuality seems to call inescapably for choices about whom and how to love. For lesbian-feminists, the threat is that bisexuals will choose a man. For heterosexuals, the threat is that bisexuals will choose a same-sex lover. For lesbians and gays, the threat is that bisexuals belie the claim that we can't help our desire. While the current rallying cry for gay rights is that of the 1950s and 1960s—namely that we have no choice, we're born this way, we can't help it—bisexuals imply that desire does not negate agency.

This does not mean that bisexuals experience desire and commitment less fully than others. Desire, affection, and other attractions do not appear for the bisexual as less intense or less commanding than they do for others—indeed, part of the pain attested to by bi writers is the product of being told to choose the appropriate partner when their desire is not so easily commanded. Nonetheless, bi people are forced into positions of choice and agency by the mutual exclusions they face. What do I do when those I live with and find community with reject my love?

Of course, some might say that we all face choices such as this. When our friends don't like our lovers we hope we won't have to choose between them, but we sometimes do. However, only rarely do such choices force a fundamental shift in one's identity. Those who find their desire and their identity firmly within lesbian parameters rarely have to change their whole identity because of their lover. Nonetheless, there are cases analogous to this one. Communities are not homogeneous wholes, but clusters of overlapping networks conveniently reified by key names. A lesbian who stops drinking may find that her identity and her friendships change quite dramatically, or a career change may move her from one network to another. These are major shifts with important implications for personal identity. They are not, however, burdened by the significance we place on sexuality. In our culture, where sexuality supposedly tells us crucial information about individuals, and where lines between sexualities and sexual communities are still strongly policed, the gender of our lover(s) defines us in spite of our personal construction of the meaning of that gender.

One response to this, of course, is to say "I am bisexual" in order to invoke a new identity and found a new community. This has been an important and often successful strategy in the 1990s, as bisexuals have fought for inclusion in lesbian and gay organizations and communities. However, instituting bisexuality as a third (or fourth) sexual identity simply expands the list of identities without building common ground or new visions for the future. It leads to the formation of LGB communities, but it does not call into question the identities contained in those initials.

Others find a more transgressive potential in bisexuality. Figured not as another sexual identity but as the negation of sexual identity, bisexuality manifests its full threat, not to lesbian or gay communities, politics, or sex, but to identity itself. As Jo Eadie says, "to say 'I am bisexual' is to say 'I am not I'" (1993, 129). If identity is secured by sexual object choice, and if bisexuality embodies a choice that is shifting and never-completed, then the position of bisexuality is indeed a position of an I that is never fully I. Bisexuals appear as "double agents" (130). We should note here not only the image of the double agent as a figure in war and politics, but the doubled agent, the agent of choice who is never self-identical. To say "I am not I" is not to say that I don't exist, or that I am not an agent, but that I am never only one, self-contained and neatly bounded. I choose, I exercise agency, but I do so not as the Enlightenment subject who knows her desires and motivations, but rather as an incomplete being in a sea of possibility.

Bisexuals appear, then, as coyote figures roaming the sexual frontier (Phelan 1996). Bisexuality, however, does not have a monopoly on this coyote identity. Transgendered people manifest double agency as well. As border figures, faithful neither to femaleness nor to maleness, trans people unmoor the "I" that is secured by gender. Faced with regimes of binary gender, trans people cross the boundary and confound life narratives. As Jacob Hale (1998) notes, this is not a matter of "high-spirited celebration or revelry," not a position of exuberance, but is a result of the fact that trans "embodiments and our subjectivities are abjected from social ontology: we cannot fit ourselves into extant categories without denying, eliding, erasing, or otherwise abjecting personally significant aspects of ourselves. . . . When we choose to live with and in our dislocatedness, fractured from social ontology, we choose to forgo intelligibility: lost in language and in social life, we become virtually unintelligible, even to ourselves" (336).

Double agents, we remember, are often disavowed by both sides and killed upon discovery. Before capture, they might well find themselves unclear at times where their loyalties lie or about how to proceed in a bipolar world. Doubled sexual agents are continually threatened by the demand to show one's papers, to declare one's allegiance, and to be recognizable to the authorities. Perhaps, however, double agents might coalesce to form non-aligned territories. How, and whether, to do that is the subject to which I now turn.

Confronting the Stranger Within

When a border zone denizen's corpse is claimed by those with firmer categorical location, border zones become less habitable for those who are trying to live in the nearly unspeakable spaces created by the overlapping margins of distinct categories. Border zone inhabitants infer reasonably that their lack of fixed location within categories is prohibited by the more firmly located, that such absence will be used as grounds for subjecting them to multiple indiscriminate erasures, and that their sullen resistant silence and their dissenting cries alike will be folded into the discourses of those with more solid categorical and thus social locations. (Hale 1998, 319)

The seriousness of the position of the double agent is often disavowed in queer theory. Despite the prominence of transgender in recent queer theory, as Prosser notes, the physical danger and emotional and ontological anguish of dislocation are often glossed over in favor of either celebrations of the frisson of dissonance or claims for the political productivity of gender trouble. If lesbians and gays are to actively attend to the situations of bi and trans people and to develop a new politics from that attention, they must include a willingness to bear that danger and that anguish.

The process of forming alliances, of acknowledging kinship with double agents or the doubling in every agent, is fraught with danger. The quest to be allies can be subverted rather than strengthened by gestures of incorporation. The inversion model assimilates sexuality into gender, making all lesbians transgendered. The assumption of fixed, exclusive sexual orientations makes bisexuals "really" lesbians or gays who won't admit it or, if in the past, didn't have the permission or privilege that would have enabled them to live as lesbian or gay. When lesbians and gays claim bisexual or transgendered people as ancestors and current members of a community against their self-understandings they do not make themselves better allies, but cannibals, as Hale describes. Claimed as lesbians or gays when that serves the purposes of those groups, disavowed when they become a source of uneasiness, bi and trans people find themselves within "LGBT communities," forced either to assimilate or to stake out more distinct territory.

Rather than consuming and subsuming bi and trans people into models of homosexuality, I suggest that we begin from the perspective of bi and trans in order to challenge traditional ideas about sexuality and gender. Bi and trans are not the same perspective by any means, but they present some similar lessons about the limitations of current lesbian and gay politics.

The first lesson of bi and trans is that sexuality is imbricated with gender, but not in any simple way. This works against both lesbian-feminist understandings, in which sexuality is about gender, and against opponents such as Gayle Rubin (1984) who argue that sexuality and gender are entirely separable (see also Rich 1980). Too much queer theory has analyzed sexuality in isolation from gender, returning us to a sort of pre-feminist homosexuality (Martin 1994). Our sexuality is always partly about gender, though not in any simple sense. Gender, conversely, is partly about sexuality. Whatever our bodily equipment, our configurations as masculine or feminine carry with them expectations about who does what, with what, with whom. We need not, however, reduce these cultural entwinements to heterosexist images of masculine beings seeking out feminine ones or homoerotic images of similar beings finding reflection and validation together. Neither should we assume that important pleasures are not derived from confounding those expectations about gender and sexuality. Recognizing that sex and gender are not isomorphic, and that neither sex nor gender is itself self-identical and clearly bounded, affords the possibility of creating new identities that are valorized, not by their "naturalness," but by their expression of agency and creativity.

The second lesson we see more clearly from the viewpoint of bi or trans thinkers is that the demand for clear boundaries and borders hurts rather than strengthens us. Boundaries appeal to our need for order, and this is a necessary part of human functioning. When we make it our life's work to defend the boundaries rather than shift them to accommodate the continually evolving excess of human life, however, we sacrifice too much to order. Boundary policing in sex and gender communities is not only authoritarian, it leads us into conceptual lacunae that are better used as inspiration. When lesbians sleep with men, sometimes the men they sleep with turn out to be FTM. Or perhaps the man is a woman (or vice versa). And maybe the lesbian is MTF, or is another kind of man. It is certainly not the job of feminists to defend boundaries and borders, to reify order; there are others who are better trained and equipped, and we will not win at that game. Our job is to continue to question boundaries, to open ourselves to the change we say we seek. Making our communities into armed camps is not good politics; rather than shoring our borders to prevent infection, we must work on infecting the body politic with the dangerous virus of irreverent democracy.

It is important to note how these "lessons" differ from forms of appropriation that cannibalize bisexuals or transgendered people. Learning lessons is an important part of democratic politics. Those who come to politics only as pre-formed subjects ready to articulate their own (pre-formed and clearly bounded) interests will never be able to explain why others should support them in their cause. The democratic articulation of interests is that process wherein people's description of their situation and their needs becomes a public matter, of concern not only to those in that situation and holding those interests but also to those with whom their fate is linked. The two lessons listed above may indeed be learned at a number of sites, but mainstream lesbian and gay politics has failed to learn or has forgotten them. Those engaged in such politics establish their commonality with the heterosexual majority by denying both the complicated relations between gender and sexuality and the ways in which the borders of lesbian and gay communities contain and bleed with many others.

The essence of appropriation is non-reciprocity. Failing to listen to and fight for others, while claiming their achievements and their pain as one's own, is not inclusion but appropriation. It is thus crucial that learning from bisexuals and transgendered people does not become a matter of claiming "we are all transsexuals" or that bisexuals are "of course" part of lesbian and gay communities while failing to attend to the specificities of different experiences. I do not offer these two lessons in order to say that we are all the same, all united in opposition to heteronormativity, but rather to suggest that we need to note the particular ways in which these general principles play out in different locations and experiences.

The first lesson suggests that the separation of sexual object choice from gender identity, the core of the construction of the modern homosexual, is both false and pernicious. Both the internal transcripts of gay and lesbian communities and the dominant heteronormative transcript have always recognized this and allowed for a multitude of links and gaps between gender and sexuality. The gay and lesbian communities' public transcript has denied it in a bid for respectability, but this denial has served only a very small group. Learning the principle of imbrication would enable the multiple groups that interpellate themselves as part of a potential community to begin to build a politics on the recognition of these imbrications as illuminating and fruitful rather than shameful.

In building such a politics, the second lesson points to a crucial element for organization and maintenance. Rather than trying to identify an agenda and a constituency a priori and then fighting to maintain the integrity of that agenda and constituency, radical sexual politics should operate through continued public discussion and negotiation about which agendas might catalyze and mobilize the broadest possible constituency. This does not mean that all groups have to affiliate with all other groups, that they must accept as allies everyone who expresses a desire to ally or makes a claim to a common agenda. The principle of porous borders should not translate into a simple command that judgments or separations are regressive. It does imply that decisions to separate or disavow others should not be based on simple identity categories, which probably fail to capture the reality of all members (and likely violate the principle established by the first lesson), but rather on statements of principle and policy about particular issues.

As a particularly thorny example, I'd like to turn to the ILGA/NAMBLA controversy of 1994. In the face of stereotypes that all gay men are pedophiles, most lesbian and gay organizations have not only disavowed groups such as the North American Man-Boy Love Association (NAMBLA) but have argued for distinguishing pedophilia from homosexuality on the grounds that heterosexuality and homosexuality designate adult orientations while pedophilia is neither heterosexual nor homosexual. This position actively resists NAMBLA's assertions of community membership and the objections of many activists to their exclusion from groups such as the International Lesbian and Gay Organization (ILGA). NAMBLA was barred from ILGA after the U.S. government made NAMBLA's membership a basis for denying non-governmental organization (NGO) status to ILGA at the United Nations. Whether such exclusion is a matter of secondary marginalization within a marginalized community or a "legitimate" distinction will not be decided by a priori definitions of community boundaries and membership but by discussions about principles and goals. If the dominant principle becomes articulated as the rights of consenting adults to love one another without discrimination, then NAMBLA will find itself out of that community. If, on the other hand, the organizing principle of a coalition or alliance is framed as the universal right to sexual freedom, then it will be much harder to justify exclusion on the grounds of age or "inappropriate object." Currently, although ILGA and its affiliated groups implicitly appeal to the principle of rights, the groups' explicit frame of identity ("lesbians and gays") leaves them continually subject to the charge that they have "turned on their own" to gain legitimacy.

The ILGA/NAMBLA case is instructive for another reason. Not only is it a case of contentious exclusion in order to buy legitimacy, it is also an example of the failure to acquire legitimacy through exclusion. After the NAMBLA expulsion, which was justified entirely by the importance of acquiring NGO status, the United States still barred ILGA. The Clinton Administration was clearly not convinced that the remaining member groups around the world were not in fact havens for perverts. Without articulated principles, ILGA was left simply with sharper, narrower boundaries. ILGA did not gain allies from the exclusion—those who opposed ILGA before continued to do so—but lost some of those who understand themselves to be part of the identity named in the organization's title and stated mission. Both those who were excluded and those who remained were disciplined just a little more, as those who remained were reminded of the boundaries of "normal" homosexuality.

When the Right comes after lesbians and gays, we who identify with or are targeted by those labels understandably fight for our right to equality. We fight for "lesbian and gay rights." We thus consolidate identities formed under duress, identities that are nonetheless rich in meaning. Yet many, if not most, lesbians and gays do not find themselves living within LGBT communities, or even in lesbian and gay communities, and they do not derive deep meaning from their sexuality except as stigma. These folks go to work, come home, engage in friendships and civic groups, and hope to be part of their home communities. For them, the point of equality is not to find validation for a particular identity, but to be what they are, to have their sexuality mean as much or as little as they choose. Making this possible involves more than demonstrating that they are as normal as their neighbors; it also requires something other than consolidating identities and adding them to a list of boundaried units deserving of rights. It requires wholesale resistance to heteronormativity and to gender tyranny, both outside and inside our communities.

Queer Communities, Queer Utopias

Susan Stryker, a transgender activist and scholar, has noted that what she finds most compelling about the idea of "queer" is "the sense of a utopian, all-encompassing point of resistance to heteronormativity and . . . a 'posthomosexual' refiguration of communities of people marginalized by sexuality, embodiment, and gender" (1998, 151). In such a refiguration, queer communities would not be bounded by initials, but would become spaces for experimentation and visioning of new possibilities for self-creation. In order for this to become possible either conceptually or in practice, however, "queer" needs to mean more than "lesbian or gay," more even than resistance and marginality. Such a starting point continues to define queer in terms of what it is not rather than in terms of its (our) own possibilities. Perhaps inevitably, queer communities will form first among those marginalized by hegemonic cultural formations; but becoming queer must involve a remapping of the social world so that marginalization, assimilation, and resistance (each of which is defined by a posited center) are all transformed into new cultural locations and forms.

   This project, of course, is not new. Throughout the nineteenth and twentieth centuries, groups of gender-variant or sexually variant people worked to create new cultures and counterpublics. The vision of queerness articulated by Stryker is a vision shared in various ways by gay liberation, lesbian-feminism, and early homosexual theorists and organizers such as Harry Hay and Edward Carpenter, as well as utopian thinkers such as Herbert Marcuse. The history of these movements and ideas illuminates the difficulties faced by such visions, as the quest for cultural autonomy is (perhaps inevitably) bound and re-bound to the hegemonic. Lesbian-feminism's attempt to produce gynocentric cultures relied, implicitly and often explicitly, on a demonization of men and masculinity (Phelan 1989; Shugar 1995). Gay liberation opened with volleys against "straight society" as well as the call to create new gay cultures. Such reaction is neither regrettable nor avoidable; the utopian drive is inescapably bound to protest against existing arrangements. Nonetheless, there are dangers in reaction. Not only is one bound emotionally, looking over one's shoulder in anger, but one is also bound conceptually. Those engaged in assimilationist projects are not the only ones who measure themselves against the dominant standard. Those engaged in countercultural programs may and do equally concern themselves with whether they "look like straights." The rejection of both bisexuals and transgendered/transsexual people has followed this pattern, as lesbians view bisexuals in terms of men rather than as creators of new possibilities, and see in trans people only the reflection of heterosexual femininity and masculinity (Raymond 1979; Rust 1995). Again, this is unavoidable to an extent: we read the new through eyes accustomed to the old, and we never see without organizing vision into patterns based on already-existing elements. Nonetheless, there are moments when, like new languages, common roots shift into new patterns and variations.

Queer should be not the banner of evasion, of some caricatured postmodern irresponsibility, but the sign of a non-identitarian utopian universalism. It is non-identitarian not in rejecting all identities, but in recognizing that no identity is self-sufficient and adequate to the job that language forces upon it. No hyphenation, no string of modifiers or extensions of identities will overcome that fundamental constitutive inadequacy. Queer communities would be those in which this inadequacy is honored and given central place rather than covered up or tolerated in the margins. Queer communities should be utopian, both in the drive for a better world and in the knowledge that the dream will never fully take shape, the day of reconciliation will never arrive. Utopianism requires a good deal of humility and patience to avoid becoming dogmatic and impractical. Finally, queer communities should be universalist, open for all, seeking to produce the values upon which everyone could find recognition and inclusion. These values cannot reduce themselves to identities, both because of the incompleteness of identity and because identity does not guarantee shared values. Much of the confusion and sense of betrayal in our communities is the result of the assumption that those with shared identities will share a sense of what those identities entail. Shared identities, however, are no substitute for shared politics. The reification of community hides this from us, but queered communities would enable us to recognize and address it. Community is not a thing or a place in which we find ourselves by birth or ascriptive attributes, but is a process by which we build commonality and difference (Phelan 1994, ch. 5). Queer community is a process of democratic values, in which lesbians and gays and trans people and bisexuals and, yes, heterosexuals participate to loosen the bonds of gender.

Would such communities be "home" to anyone? By this I mean to ask, not whether anyone would be eligible for membership, but rather whether such communities would provide the stability and belonging that humans (even postmodern ones) need. Prosser's insistence that sexual difference is a persistent and basic feature of human societies, and that crossings as well as fixity sustain this difference, is well taken. The bonds of gender are experienced very differently for different sorts of people: for some they are a burden and a constriction, for others (very often trans people) they are a crucial support for personal identity and self-esteem. Loosening the bonds of gender cannot mean, then, a forced regime of resistance to assignment, as lesbian-feminists such as Jeffreys (1997) seem to advocate, but loosening the demand to be recognizable *or not*, as well as prior understandings of what one's partner(s) reveals about one's gender identity or political or cultural commitments. Such a community, I believe, could indeed be a home: not a hall of mirrors, reflecting oneself back consistently, but a place where one could be recognized as a person with both a history and a future that has not yet been written.

Attempts to valorize our sexual identities, to give ourselves legitimacy through constructing histories or making claims to our superior nature or culture, always work by excluding important people and questions. Mainstream lesbians and gays have hidden bisexuals because they seem to present the possibility that we could be straight if we wanted. But there is no pleasure in a movement based on the claim that we can't help it. Imagine, instead, a movement to foster agency and variety in sexuality. Feminists have spearheaded such movements, but these movements have too often been contained at points where we are forced to confront our own fears and abjections. But forming real BTLG communities would mean pushing past the discomfort to the place of creativity. In this place we could ask one another, Who lives inside of you? What do those selves dream of and desire? How can we do justice to all of them? Silencing bi and trans people is part of the silencing of all of us—the butches who can't admit to the boys and men (and little girls and hot babes) in them, the femmes who fear for their feminist credentials, the androgynes who long for other androgynes, the lesbian-feminists who get hot talking politics, and all the others inside and around us.

Beliefs that bisexuals are unreliable or that MTF or FTM lesbians are agents of patriarchy rest on an ideology born of fear and despair. It is time to abandon those parents and move with the knowledge that citizenship will not be bought by drawing new boundaries. We also have to challenge our fears, to consider seriously that the certainty about our identities that citizenship seems to offer comes at the cost of falsifying and denying the strangeness within each of us, of every sexuality. This is not a step into equality, but a renunciation for which we will all pay dearly.

Queering Citizenship

n democratic regimes, minorities can only change the rules if they persuade a substantial number of the majority that such changes are justified. Such changes are often fleeting and imperfect; we should not read every piece of legislation as reflecting perfectly the mood of the people at that time. Still, we can be confident that laws will endure only if they find reasonable accord with the population. Thus, citizenship for some depends upon the willingness of the majority to acknowledge them as members. This willingness in turn depends upon the construction of a new hegemony, with new readings of rights, equality, and membership.

Overlooking the role of acknowledgment has led several scholars to assert recently that acting as a citizen—whether through voting or participation in electoral politics, demonstrations, or cultural strategies of visibility and confrontation—is sufficient for establishing one's citizenship. Rightly noting that such action is essential to the idea of citizens as political actors rather than targets of policy, authors such as Lauren Berlant (1997) have stated or implied that such action is sufficient for citizenship regardless of the response of others. But citizenship and its practices cannot take place in a vacuum. Whether an action fosters citizenship depends upon the interplay between the actor and those with and toward whom s/he acts. It is never a matter simply between individuals or even between groups, but is a contest among and within polities concerning the constitution of those polities. Since citizenship is an element, perhaps the central element, in modern political constructions of the "we," its parameters and limits describe the polity's sense of itself. Although dissent may be an important vehicle for expressing citizenship, dissent in the face of total rejection is not citizenship but rebellion. Such rebellion becomes citizenship not simply when the rebel claims to be a member of the polity, but when other members of that polity recognize her as such. This is not an all-or-nothing proposition: no polity of any complexity will be unanimous in its judgments, including cultural judgments about who is "really" a member. But we can use the concept of acknowledgment to evaluate whether and how particular polities incorporate diversities of various sorts, and how far that incorporation leads those polities to transform their dominant self-understandings. Whether and in what ways a polity is open to change can be signaled not only by who is allowed to hold office, but by how they are enabled or prevented from transforming public meanings. Queer citizenship will also be the emergence of major change in the American polity. Whether the citizenship of lesbians and gays will make such a difference is less clear.

In order to make good on such sweeping claims, I will return here to several dilemmas of citizenship that have been visited in earlier chapters. Precisely because they are partially constitutive of modern citizenship, conceptions of bodies and kinship must be challenged if citizenship is to become open to all. These conceptions also point to avenues for alliances with overlapping or "other" groups. They also give substance to the distinction between "lesbian and gay" and "queer," a distinction that has become increasingly important not only in political action but in controversies over the goals of such action. At the same time, the process of queering must extend into a deconstruction of the binary between these terms as well; as I argued in Chapter 4, a too-neat dichotomy between these both obscures the destabilizing moment in even modest proposals for change and ignores the participation of queer politics in prevailing American norms of individualism and self-expression. The question, then, is not "queer or not," or "how to make citizenship queer," but how to queer citizenship—how to continue the subversion of a category that is nonetheless both crucial and beneficial for millions of people around the world. We may thus expect to find not only that the patriarchal and phallic foundations of citizenship must be chipped away, but that the modes in which we have thought about political membership are also not up to the task of re-imagining. Reaching this conclusion is not a cause for despair, but rather provokes the beginning in the middle that is all human action.

Straight Democracy

The contemporary project of equality for lesbians and gays has appealed to heterosexuals on the basis of two intertwined claims. First, activists invoke the American promise of freedom and equality, specifically the freedom to build one's own life on the basis of one's own values rather than in deference to traditional authority. Thus, equality for sexual minorities is presented as a simple extension of existing American ideals. The second claim concerns what it means to be gay or lesbian. Essentialist arguments have been much more effective in convincing heterosexual Americans to support equal rights because they fit the more recent American ethos that one should not be penalized for "being who one is," that "merit" (defined in terms of academic or job-related performance) should overcome "prejudice." These arguments suggest that gay rights is part of the neutral procedural republic so fondly imagined by liberal theorists.

As we have seen, contemporary gay authors and political organizations have paired these arguments to make lesbians and gays more recognizable to heterosexuals as "like themselves," hard-working Americans who want and deserve a "normal American life." We have also seen the costs of this strategy, not only for lesbians and gays who don't look normal enough, but also for bisexuals and transgendered people. Procedural liberalism's claim to neutrality can hold only when the differences in question are seen as not making a difference, not really changing the polity. Those whose difference does make a difference continue to find themselves left out, abandoned not only by heterosexuals but by those gays and lesbians who do not want their difference to make a difference.

Political theory has mirrored these problems. Because contemporary democratic theorists have either ignored sexual diversity, have modeled it on racial, ethnic, or national diversity, or have implicitly essentialized it, when they consider gays and lesbians at all they offer forms of inclusion that do not address the larger problem of strangeness. Before considering what queering citizenship might look like, it is worth while to look briefly at what it cannot be.

Recent treatments of citizenship have tried to steer a republican path that is appropriate for contemporary, diverse polities. Comparing schemes for resolution of conflict, Benjamin Barber (1984) contrasts "strong democracy" with both the "thin" democracy of liberalism and the "unitary" democracy of communitarianism. Thin democracy is characterized by bargaining among privately focused interest groups and individuals, by a reliance on the law and the courts to arbitrate social disagreement and protect individual rights, and by minimal citizen participation in politics. In contrast, unitary democracy calls on individuals to identify with the community to such an extent that they cannot resist it. It sees conflict as pathological and consensus as the desired goal of politics. We read here the same dilemma that is elsewhere labeled "liberal versus communitarian." Neither option is truly political, in that both ignore crucial aspects and prerequisites of political life: liberals frame everything in terms of individual rights, seeing politics as an instrument to law, and communitarians refuse the full flavor of conflict that is a part of any real public encounter.

Barber's conception of strong democracy is a republican model. He defines strong democracy as "politics in the participatory mode where conflict is resolved in the absence of an independent ground through a participatory process of ongoing, proximate self-legislation and the creation of a political community capable of transforming dependent, private individuals into free citizens and partial and private interests into public goods" (132). Strong democracy emphasizes bonds between citizens while making clear that these civic bonds cannot be reduced to ascriptive categories such as ethnicity, and stressing the transformation of private interest in the face of public processes. It thus focuses on the creation of a public sphere, a sphere missing from both liberalism and communitarianism.

Within this arena, political agents are constituted through participation in debate, deliberation, struggle, and decision. As Barber describes it, "strong democracy creates the very citizens it depends upon *because* it depends upon them, because it permits the representation neither of *me* nor of we, because it mandates a permanent confrontation between the *me* as citizen and the 'Other' as citizen, forcing us to think in common and act in common" (153). Thus, strong democratic citizenship entails a commitment to publicity, to dialogue and debate, and to the preconditions for these to be meaningful. The latter include not only the elimination of legal barriers, but the range of social supports that enable people to develop their powers of body, intellect, and emotion so that they have the ability to form and defend opinion, face up to conflict, and reach toward others without abandoning their own ideas and beliefs. These needs will not all be provided by the state; most will not be. But the activities of citizens are not targeted only toward the state, nor need they occur within a single, undifferentiated "public sphere"; "the public" is the name for a multiplicity of arenas in which citizens create a common future.

Many critics have challenged Barber's proposals. Iris Marion Young (1990, 1995) has cogently argued that Barber's republicanism contains the oppositions and assumptions that have limited access and distorted the struggles of oppressed peoples. She notes his confident distinction between the public and the private, his preference for the common (i.e., the "public") over the particular (the "private"), and his prioritization of the "public" identity of citizenship over other social and political identities. She points out that dreams of universality "tend to exclude or to put at a disadvantage some groups, even when they have formally equal citizenship status" (1995, 182). And, crucially, she notes Barber's "confusion between plurality and privatization" (183) that makes him unable to clearly differentiate between issues and identities grounded in new social movements and liberal interest-group formations.

I agree with Young's assessment of Barber. Barber cannot understand the "we" as anything but a "we" that centers him, and his strong democracy does not answer the questions and fears of those who will always be minorities in that "we." However, Young's call for "a group differentiated citizenship" (1995, 184) is not an improvement over Barber's public sphere. Young argues that justice and equality require direct representation of oppressed groups (Young 1990). She proposes such differential representation as a means to overcome the marginalization and powerlessness of underrepresented groups, and she argues that the dynamics of oppression make it impossible for members of dominant groups to adequately represent the oppressed. The presence of social groups and political actors identified with those groups is indeed necessary if public spheres are not to be arenas of false universality. Young's answer, however, has also come under fire (and indeed it is unclear whether Young would endorse these proposals today). Given that "sexual orientation," "race," and "gender" are not biological absolutes but complex historical constructions whose meaning and boundaries differ over time, we might justly fear that such allocations will both fail to capture the diversity of needs and views within groups and will reify categories that are continually in flux (as demonstrated, for example, by the growing resistance of multiracial Americans to racial categories on the census and other forms).

Young's hope that such representation would indeed be able to represent the needs, perspectives, and interests of the members of a group must also be questioned. The first obstacle is the fact of diversity among gays and lesbians, a diversity no greater or less than that existing within any group. Such diversity will always put the lie to any attribution of representativeness on the part of particular persons. It is in fact part of the dynamic of stigmatization that stigmatized groups must endure "representatives" rather than being individuals. Second, representation inescapably encounters the problem of the "professionalization" of representatives. As Erving Goffman (1963, 26) describes this process, "native leaders are obliged to have dealings with representatives of other categories, and so find themselves breaking out of the closed circle of their own kind." In turn, the representatives gradually become less representative of the people they represent. Indeed, Goffman notes that "from the beginning such leaders may be recruited from those members of the category who are ambitious to leave the life of its members and relatively able to do so" (ibid.). Goffman's observation demonstrates why we should be suspicious of attempts to represent groups by counting heads. This dilemma does not mean that we should not care whether lesbians and gays are present in legislation or policy fora. It means that the voice of particular individuals cannot be taken to speak for "their group" in general. I cannot imagine a political process, or a sufficiently small scale of organization, that would obviate this problem.

In fact, Young's proposal for group representation replicates the problems of republicanism, albeit on a smaller scale. Where Barber assumes the possibility of a coherently unified citizenry, Young assumes the possibility of a coherently unified social group. Challenging the false generality of republican visions is important work, but it cannot be replaced by other false generalities. Fully accepting plurality means living with structures that fail to capture all, or all of everyone's, concerns. The plural grounds of the public must be directed sometimes to the multiplication of voices rather than their organization. The goal of this multiplication is not a larger "marketplace of ideas" in which the best will win, or simply a space for a thousand flowers to bloom, but rather the formation of new hegemonic blocs that can produce changes in the lives of people. Group representations—quotas, if you will—make sense in some sorts of allocational schemes for certain goods, but such representation in governmental institutions (especially existing ones) is more likely to generate new splits and exclusions (and to let the majority off the hook) than to bring about major change.

Any hopes for representation encounter a further diliemma in the case of "invisible minorities" such as (most) lesbians and gays. Representation is further complicated by the incentives to disavow one's difference. This points to the final problem with political representation at this point: absent the cultural change that will make sexual strangers able to be secure as members of the polity, only a small and unrepresentative group will be willing to be identified as such. Political, legal, and cultural change combine in unpredictable ways to incite one another, so we cannot say one sort of change must precede another to be effective; we can, however, say that there will be limits to the effectiveness of political changes that are not accompanied by cultural ones (if those changes indeed can occur at all).

If Barber offers us a straight democracy, one that in fact avoids pressing questions about cultural diversity and privilege, he is not alone. Citizenship has always been the riskiest terrain for difference. All the metaphors and expectations of citizenship—membership, equality, acknowledgment, reciprocity—return us to the imagined horizon where we face one another as recognizable and deserving not only of respect but also of shared power. Is it possible to retain the promise of citizenship without flattening differences, either from without or from within groups? What would we require to fulfill such a promise?

Citizenship for sexual minorities cannot mean simply being included under heterosexual rules, either as disembodied persons or as a clearly marked minority. Neither option fully challenges the heterosexual state. The republican strategy overlooks difference, while the minority option makes too much of it. As strangers, gays and lesbians are literally everywhere: dispersed randomly throughout communities, without a clearly different culture or language, with differences whose impact is only beginning to be understood. This provides social theorists with an exciting opportunity to move from examining the problems of a minority to considering the sexual structure of modern societies. It calls for us to reexamine the "we" rather than focus narrowly on a "they" who don't fit the norm.

Linda Nicholson has recently made this point. In her critique of Charles Taylor's "politics of recognition" (Taylor 1994), Nicholson (1999) notes the essentialism that haunts (North) American politics. Nicholson demonstrates that Taylor's discussion proceeds from the assumption of a neat line between "we" and "other," ignoring the reality of overlapping memberships and shifting interpellations. Taylor frames the question of multiculturalism as a matter of minorities demanding that majorities recognize their moral worth. Certainly that has been one element of all civil rights and equality struggles. It is not, however, the only element. The "more challenging voices" that Taylor (and Barber) ignores are "those saying, 'Let my presence make you more aware of the limitations of what you have so far judged to be true and of worth'" (Nicholson 1999, 138). Against the weaker demand for recognition, which he endorses, Taylor reads this challenge as a matter of power over reason, relativism without end. But as Nicholson argues, reading the challenge this way is an indication not of the relativism of the challengers but of Taylor's inability to see beyond his own horizon. It demonstrates the point at which even those Stanley Fish (1999) calls "strong multiculturalists" cannot or will not allow the presence of other cultures or identities to shape their identities or goals in turn. While difference here is admitted to make a difference, it cannot reshape the self-conceptions of the dominant group—the difference remains on the side of the other.

Citizenship for strangers must entail a recognition of the strangeness of citizens if it is to be more than a colonization of subjugated cultures.

As the equal membership of lesbians and gays in the polity and civil society, citizenship requires the construction of a solidaristic ethos between sexual minorities and the heterosexual majority. This solidarity is not to be confused with assimilation or simple toleration. It requires an active encounter with difference and a willingness to understand differences as fruitful and enhancing rather than as threats to bodily, social, or political integrity. In some instances, such as the problems of anti-gay violence and military service, such encounters may lead to inclusion and equal protection under the laws. In others, such as marriage, solidaristic encounters may offer new ways to conceptualize institutions, to offer a range of affiliations to all citizens. Without such solidarity, however, legal equality will remain empty. It will either be a facade masking continued exclusion, or it will be procedural inclusion enforced by the state but lacking social legitimacy.

State/Citizenship

Because citizenship is a political category, activists and theorists are likely to look to state apparatuses for its achievement or transformation. The membership needs of citizens cannot all be addressed by state venues, however, so an exclusive focus on the state will always be a mistake. This does not mean that any encounter with the state is a mistake. Legal challenges and legislative campaigns are not simply instrumental but also serve as sites of organization for broader community goals. It must be made clear, however, that such campaigns do not automatically produce public spaces; without a concerted effort at long-term community building, these campaigns can instead sap the energies of a group with little long-term result. Thus, lesbians and gays must focus on infrastructure as well as issue campaigns. Rights, however extensive, are not the sum of the definition of citizenship; or rather, rights can only become real in people's lives when they are sufficiently supported culturally to be exercised. As the history of African-Americans demonstrates, legal rights without cultural and political support are simply the facade of rights.

The drive for rights may at times in fact run counter to citizenship strategies. This is not a defect in rights, but reflects limited legalistic understandings of the place of rights in people's lives. Seen as private possessions rather than as the vehicle and mode of communal membership, rights become the sum of citizenship. As formal rights are granted (the right to be "like us"), resistance grows toward any further considerations of the shape of the polity, such as social and economic patterns of discrimination. As the guarantor of individual liberty, rights seem to level the playing field and to leave the outcome to the individual. Further consideration of the "we" is deemed either moralistic (if done by the Right) or whiny (if done by the Left). Thus, the public nature of citizenship, the binding of members to one another, is refused in a politics of rights alone.

Citizenship is also limited by strategies of change that rely simply on the lobbying or legal efforts of national organizations. Such organizations rely primarily on small staffs of professionals, who are paid to lobby or organize on behalf of "the community." The organizations that purport to represent gays and lesbians have no local chapters, no conventions, no elections of their boards. The involvement of most members is limited to writing checks (Vaid 1995, 223). This does not mean that such organizations do not serve a purpose, but rather that their purposes are limited. Citizenship strategies must combine legislative and judicial campaigns with social activism and education. In the absence of real changes of ideas and opinions, today's legal efforts will be eroded as soon as our opponents organize. This organization is already visible in the legislation passed by Congress and many state legislatures that denies validation of any same-sex marriages that might be performed in their own or other states.

Acknowledgments of citizenship are embedded within social structures that afford recognition and reciprocity among members of a polity. Without such recognition and reciprocity, formal guarantees of protection and rights are fragile and unintelligible to many. There is no shortcut to equality or liberty; they must be fought for, not just in state houses but in media representations, news coverage, local and community affairs, financial and economic structures, and daily life. The greatest danger of a narrowed focus for activism is the conceit that legal admission to a few select institutions constitutes citizenship. Citizenship requires acknowledgment and inclusion in institutions, but it also requires a public culture of acknowledgment.

If citizenship is to be more than a "right to certain privileges"

(Ignatieff 1995), it requires the patience to build grassroots structures and the determination to confront the arguments against equal membership. Focusing on legislation when the culture does not offer lesbians and gays the real promise of equality will perhaps inevitably foster interest-group strategies over citizenship strategies. In so doing, activists run the risk of losing the battle for citizenship by fighting for rights. As a goal, citizenship has less to do with bundles of goods than with public acknowledgment as a member. The demand for citizenship is also a promise to undergo the risks and burdens facing members of that society, to unite one's fate with that of one's fellow citizens. As such, it militates against quick fixes or narrow visions of self-interest.

A further question for state-centered strategies concerns whether and how political actors will be motivated to include sexual minorities. Struggles for inclusion are shaped not only by the needs of the excluded and the fears or needs of the excluders, not only by whether demands can be framed within the rhetoric of the polity, but by whether state actors have an incentive to include the excluded. The incentives of those actors will not only affect whether a group is included, but will importantly shape the terms under which inclusion will occur. Those terms may not always be ones most advantageous to the excluded group. Thus, if they are not to replicate structures of exclusion and privilege among themselves, those who aspire to citizenship must understand their situation within the larger context of state institutions, national culture(s), and intragroup differences of need and perspective.

John Dryzek (1996) has considered whether group interests can be addressed through state-centered strategies. He offers two criteria for evaluating the prospects for a given change. First is the extent to which the group's interests "can be assimilated to any state imperative" (484). If the interests are peripheral to state imperatives, the group is likely to be forced to limit its own concerns in order to fit within dominant understandings, and it will achieve little more than symbolic gains. The second question is "whether the group's entry into the state would leave behind a flourishing civil society" (485). If not, then the group must consider that its larger and long-term interests will not be not served by such strategies. A recent example illuminates this point. The battle to pass a civil rights bill in Massachusetts was conducted largely through a strategy that avoided the involvement of gays and lesbians (Cicchino,

Deming, and Nicholson 1995). Rather than conduct a campaign of education and activism, members of the Massachusetts Gay and Lesbian Political Caucus worked with legislators as quietly as possible, hoping to fly under the radar of opponents. Not only was the product of this campaign seriously defective, failing to challenge homophobia and ignorance; its anti-political interest-group strategy thwarted the possibilities for citizenship in favor of getting some goods. Rather than building solidarity, it fractured minority communities and failed to challenge heterosexual understandings.

Dryzek's questions are extremely cogent and useful for evaluating the prospects for gay and lesbian membership. Before addressing them, however, it is worthwhile to disaggregate "the state." The experience of racial minorities, women, and, to an extent, lesbians and gays indicates that we can usefully distinguish legislative from judicial imperatives and strategies. I will argue that although many interests of lesbian and gay citizens may be advanced through the courts, a focus on citizenship is more properly addressed to legislatures and civil society.

In the United States and elsewhere, lesbians and gays are currently in an ambiguous position. The interests of sexual minorities present at best a distraction from state imperatives, and at worst a target for opponents. Gays and lesbians serve as one of the foci for right-wing organizers in a post–Cold War world, substituting for Communism. Legislative supporters of equality are increasing, yet they have failed so far to successfully attach demands for equality to other state concerns. President Clinton's total rejection of gays and lesbians in the 1996 election is a recent striking example of the results of such isolation. This is not simply a story of a deceitful, insincere candidate who used the hopes of group and abandoned its concerns and needs when things got tough (though it may be that). At this writing, the 2000 election campaigns are underway, and the Democratic candidates are increasingly reaching out to lesbian and gay communities for votes. Their desire for those votes, however, is not so secure that they will stick with positions they articulate, even for a week. Any opposition to proposals causes them to retract or "redefine" their remarks. Any candidate can and will take this route precisely because the concerns facing lesbian and gay citizens are easily isolable from state priorities and mandates, and lesbians and gays are perceived to have no alternatives. In such a condition, the heterosexual candidate/legislator holds all the cards. Gays and lesbians may try to get "in" and may, depending on the political actor they confront, feel more or less successful, but they do not have the leverage needed to make their presence inviting to those in power. The dynamics of such a situation lean toward assimilation or silence rather than power and equality.

Dryzek's second criterion, the effect that a group's entrance into the state has on the vitality of civil society, also has no clear answer in this case. Certainly the last decade has seen an explosion of gay public discourse, media representations, and cultural influence. This growth is not, however, a product of state action nor is it strengthened significantly by it. There has been no clear link between, for example, nondiscrimination laws and the level of cultural visibility and activity in a given state. Until recently, neither New York nor California had nondiscrimination laws (although certain municipalities had ordinances). And indeed, most such laws are underutilized when instituted because many gays and lesbians would rather not "make an issue" out of their sexuality in public. For the same reason, companies and municipalities with domestic-partner legislation have found that enrollments are lower than expected. Of course, some of this is no doubt due to the fact that many partners have insurance through their own jobs; but because claiming such benefits entails coming out at work, many continue to face a difficult choice. The existence of such laws does not protect sexual strangers from the social stigma that difference brings, even when certain manifestations are barred. Thus we cannot conclude that state engagement has strengthened civil society among lesbians and gays. We can be sure, however, that it has not harmed it. As we saw in Chapter 4, the range of political and social views and fora for their expression has grown exponentially over the 1990s. This growth has resulted in increasing political power in some areas of the country, but that power remains sharply limited.

The threat to nascent civil society from engagement with the state lies more in the possibilities for silencing and alienating the very activists who worked over the last fifty years to build such a formation. As mainstream organizations grow, and as neoconservative gay authors gain regular public fora not only among gays but in mainstream media outlets, the leftist and iconoclastic views that made such entry possible are increasingly denounced as infantile, unrealistic, or distracting. Thus, the subaltern counterpublics of the 1950s to the 1980s, including lesbian-feminists, gay liberationists, socialists, queers of color, and gender rebels are giving way to a glossy civil society of guppie/luppie magazines, vacation packages, party apparatchiks, and would-be players in the truncated arena of American politics. As the visible political spectrum of gays and lesbians becomes that of heterosexual America, a case can be made that civil society is dying even as it seems to grow. Or perhaps it is simply an indication that "civil society," like all overarching concepts, is too blunt a tool to assess recent developments. Dryzek's assumption of neatly bounded groups with their own clearly marked civil societies cannot account for the variety within and between apparently bounded groups. A socialist counterpublic remains, and various queer ones are developing, although they are now counter not only to heterosexuals but to most lesbians and gays. Clearly, we cannot answer Dryzek's question with a neat yes or no.

I have argued throughout this book that these recent developments are not simply matters of progress, nor are they evidence of failure. Rather, they are part of the process by which sexual strangers have come to seek entry and end their status as strangers. This quest, I have suggested, is fundamentally flawed. It is flawed not because rights are not important, not because acknowledgment is not vital or because citizenship is an unworthy goal, but because the current structures of citizenship are inextricably bound with the generation of strangers. Attempts to acquire citizenship without changing the construction of citizenship that prevails in the United States will fail, and they will harm our most vulnerable members in the process. The question to ask of state-centered strategies right now is not whether to engage the state, but what sort of citizenship is worth fighting for. That is, rather than starting by asking what the state can give to queers, we need to start by asking how citizenship needs to be queered if strangers are to find a home. The demand that heterosexuals learn about themselves by enlarging their perspective to include us must be accompanied by a willingness to show our queerness, to them and to one another. Of course, those gays and lesbians who feel themselves to be just like (which?) heterosexuals will not want to participate in such a project; but those of us who don't fit the new image, who are too butch or too femme or too confusing or too "wrong" somehow, need them. Just as sexual minorities in general need the solidarity of heterosexuals to create change, the queers among sexual minorities need the "model citizens" to understand and defend those differences. This is not a matter of identity politics simpliciter, of saying to some that they are "really queer" and so their interests lie with the queerest among them; it is a matter of principled support for sexual and gender variance. As conduits between the queerest and the heterosexuals, model citizens should challenge rather than emphasize their difference from bisexuals, transgendered people, or "flaming" queers.

What, then, is this queering of citizenship that we all need?

Queer Citizens

The central disruption of queer theory has been to challenge the limits of identities and the tensions that necessarily come into play as we use identity categories in political discourse. As Judith Butler (1993, 227) notes, although "it is necessary to assert political demands through recourse to identity categories, and to lay claim to the power to name oneself and determine the conditions under which that name is used, it is also impossible to sustain that kind of mastery over the trajectory of those categories within discourse." The attempt to conceptualize lesbian and gay sexualities as "social and cultural forms in their own right" must always be burdened with the recognition that such specificity does not confer semiotic self-determination in the realm of the social within which such forms arise.

Alexander Doty (1993) notes the paradoxical quality of queerness when he describes distinctions between "queer/queerness and lesbian/ lesbianism (or gay/gayness, bisexual/bisexuality)" as "attempts to mediate between the impulse to deconstruct established sexual and gender categories and the feeling that these categories need to be considered because they represent important cultural and political positions" (xvi). As Doty puts it, "queer" describes "the non-straight work, positions, pleasures, and readings of people who either don't share the same 'sexual orientation' as that articulated in the texts they are producing or responding to (the gay man who takes queer pleasure in a lesbian sitcom narrative, for example), or who don't define themselves as lesbian, gay, bisexual (or straight, for that matter)" (xviii).

In this sense, "queer" functions as a term within a discourse that we can describe, following Eve Sedgwick (1990), as "universalizing." By this term, Sedgwick refers to a view in which the definition and demarcation of the homosexual/heterosexual binary is not just an issue for those placed on the homosexual side (the minoritizing strategy) but is "an issue of continuing, determinative importance in the lives of people across the spectrum of sexualities" (1). By challenging the boundary lines as well as the content of the territories that they mark, queer work calls each of us, of any sexuality, to attend to the uncertainties and incompletions in our identities. In this sense, queer signifies "the open mesh of possibilities, gaps, overlaps, dissonances and resonances, lapses and excesses of meaning when the constituent elements of anyone's gender, of anyone's sexuality aren't made (or can't be made) to signify monolithically" (Sedgwick 1993, 8). As we attend to these gaps, the inescapable incompletions in our social spaces become visible as well, incompletions that offer the renewed chance of democratic politics.

These gaps are the zones of strangers. In complex modern societies, in which "locals" themselves do not have a clear place anymore, the role of the stranger does not diminish but grows. More and more of us are strangers, even in our "native" communities. This does not bring cosmopolitan appreciation of contingency and ambiguity, however, but heightens fears for identity and security. Thus, in the United States we see a simultaneous increase in the expressions of acceptance for homosexuality and in the backlash against the visibility of gays and lesbians. The instability of the figure of the stranger invites a slippage into the rhetoric of the enemy, as the recent "culture wars" have made clear. From a position of hegemony so complete that it need not be stated, heterosexuality now emerges as one possible sexual orientation; and fears that without total prohibition of homosexuality the population will cease to reproduce or function suggest the elusive power of the stranger as well as the militancy of the enemy.

We may see the contrast between earlier and later hegemonies by comparing contemporary lesbian and gay visibility with that of the 1950s. The 1950s in the United States was a time of nascent organizing by lesbians and gays, with several new publications and organizations that eventually laid the groundwork for later changes. This was not the source of their visibility at the time, however. Rather, they were in the news because they were the targets of criminal investigations ranging from bar raids to U.S. Senate hearings into "sexual deviants" in the State Department (Blasius and Phelan 1997; D'Emilio 1983). Any concerns for the civil rights of U.S. citizens were muted or eliminated in the overwhelming fears of invasion and corruption. Homosexuality appeared in the news simply as a problem for "the public" to address. There were no homosexual subjects, only objects of policy.

By the 1990s, several decades of organizing and activism had drastically changed matters. Still vilified by many, homosexuals now not only kept government jobs, they ran for office (often successfully), demanded equal rights, and sought and gained media visibility as subjects in their own right. In such an atmosphere the presumptive, formerly implicit heterosexuality of the citizen body must be made explicit and fought for. Competing discourses figure homosexuals alternately as citizens and as threats, or sometimes both at once—the citizen who demands more citizenship than others, whose excessive citizenship endangers that of heterosexuals. The very emergence of heterosexuality as a political identity, as something the majority must become aware of and reflect upon (even if only by refusing to reflect), is both symptomatic of the success of gay and lesbian activism and part of the backlash against that success. As heterosexuals lose the privilege of the "native" and become "strangers to themselves" (Kristeva 1991), they are forced to participate in the self-consciousness from which they had heretofore been exempted. Then queer citizens will not be differentiated by "sexual orientation," but by their recognition of strangeness in themselves and excitement at encountering it in others. Rather than a solidarity based on principles that "anyone" might agree to, queer citizens will recognize the incompleteness of principles and the importance of specificities, which never constitute a complete description.

Queer Citizenship

Optimists might conclude that such extensions of strangeness will begin to transform contemporary citizenship itself. Certainly that is one possibility. As more people begin to confront strangeness not simply as "not fitting" a particular regime by virtue of stigmatized identities but as an existential condition of modernity, we might expect demands for "slack in the order" and new understandings of political membership. The success of these demands is not, however, a given; the violent reactions to modernity and its ambivalences around the world are proof that it is more likely to generate new fundamentalisms and exclusions. As William Connolly (1995, xii) notes, pluralization and fundamentalization are twins, in that "each drive to pluralization is countered by a fundamentalism that claims to be authorized by a god or by nature." Further, he cautions, "any drive to pluralization can itself be fundamentalized" when those seeking pluralization escape political contest (or their own uncertainties) by claiming an authorization such as god or nature. Those who cannot confront strangeness in others are no more likely to welcome it in themselves. More likely is the birth of new memberships (such as heterosexuality) and the grafting of new ones onto old (for example, the patriotic homosexual citizen). These grafts are not simple assimilation (if any assimilation is simple), but neither are they direct challenges to or transformations of existing regimes.[1] The changes wrought by lesbian and gay challenges will depend upon their reception by heterosexuals and the extent to which these challenges transform heterosexual ways of life and meanings, including the idea of citizenship. But such changes will not occur if sexual minorities resist pluralization in favor of a bland pluralism that reinforces boundaries and limits.

If the model citizen remains phallic, then the imposition of other identities is virtually guaranteed to be experienced as a wound and an attack. Bypassing the phallic citizen is essential for the citizenship of lesbians and gays, as well as the citizenship of people of color and all women. The continuing association of citizenship with the (implicitly) white masculine (but not too masculine) body, and the cluster of demands and fears created by the ideology of that body as invulnerable, have conspired in racist and sexist arguments against equality. They have also led to rejection of the more public presentation and legitimation of emotion, whether politicians crying or same-sex couples holding hands, on the grounds that such public emotion is too "private" or "subjective" to be a basis for common life (Nicholson 1999, 155). Such critics, many of whom adhere to the ideals of an older leftism, reject feminism and other new social movements in terms that are remarkably reminiscent of right-wing critics of "feminization" or the "softening" of the body politic.[2] In response, those seeking entry have either claimed to be or have masqueraded as phallic agents. Not only does this response force many to deny their specificities of culture and sensibility; the anxieties and resentments of phallic citizenship constitute a price in and of themselves.

Different groups necessarily confront the specter of phallic citizenship from different angles. Because the process of group construction and maintenance is shot through with norms and narratives about the history, identity, and culture of the group (norms and narratives produced both by "group members" and those who are "outside" the group), no single response can be expected within even the most apparently neatly bounded community. For some, phallic citizenship will appear not only attractive, but as a natural extension of their current self-understandings; gay conservatives might be expected to be found here, but they will have many unexpected bedfellows. For others, phallic citizenship appears as a tragic farce that violates their integrity and solidarity with others. In spite of citizenship's origins in notions of fraternity and civic consciousness, contemporary phallic citizenship is not truly about relations with others except as obstacles. The phallic citizen and the wounded consumer are twins, looking out for themselves in a hostile world. Aspiring to such a citizenship might well seem to some to be a flight from others rather than entry and acknowledgment in a community.

The phallic citizen is not the only barrier to citizenship for sexual strangers. As we have seen, the imbrication of kinship and citizenship, and the heterosexual formulation of kinship that defines gays and lesbians (as well as unmarried adults) as either outside kin networks or unable to form new ones, suggests that kinship will have to be rethought as well. While the larger project of changing kinship is well beyond my expertise and my intentions here, a few remarks are in order.

If one of the strengths of communitarian thought has been its insistence on accounting for the contexts in which people live and make sense of their lives, a corresponding weakness has been a tendency to reify those contexts and the understandings they have produced. The step from noting our need for communities of meaning that are not simply voluntary to treating particular communities as inevitable, "natural," or beneficial to all their members is a small one, one that has been made by communitarians throughout the 1980s and 1990s (cf. Etzioni 1995). It is precisely such thinking that has reserved marriage for heterosexuals on the grounds that we've always done it this way, we (heterosexuals) gain important meaning and identity through this, so opening marriage to "same-sex" couples would be a violation not of rights, but of a way of life. The willingness of some opponents of same-sex marriage to consider domestic partnership casts queer couples as liberal contractors, like business partners, with rights carefully circumscribed to prevent encroachment on dominant meanings. Opponents fear both that partnership is "too much like marriage," therefore threatening the heterosexual status of that institution, and that it represents the encroachment of liberal contract on communities.

Queering kinship will not require same-sex marriage. If anthropologists are to be believed (and I see no reason not to believe them), current American notions of family rely on intergenerational "blood" ties for their center. Marriage is less central in that formulation than such ties. This is precisely why adoption and parenting are the most contentious elements of marriage and partnership debates. Nonetheless, marriage remains a key concept for legitimating and privileging certain relationships. Extending the right of marriage to same-sex couples will indeed change cultural assumptions about who may and does love whom, about the meaning of reproductivity and parenting. This does not mean, however, that it will deeply change assumptions about the relations between kinship and citizenship. By extending an institution that feminists and others have widely identified as a linchpin of patriarchy (even as this institution is under attack for other economic and social reasons), we run the risk of reconsolidating the idea of the responsible citizen as economically independent (or at least married to a provider), thus removing the burden of notice and care from other citizens. If tax law and insurance benefits simply recognize the new households, citizenship will not change in any significant way (although certainly the cultural life and the daily lives of citizens would be importantly different).

If same-sex marriage will not queer citizenship, what sorts of kinship changes might? The primary change needed is the erosion of the idea of kin relations as the only people upon whom one may legitimately call for aid in times of need. The public/private split so extensively challenged by feminists includes the expectation that "private" connections between people are more real and rich than "public" ones. This expectation has grown over the last twenty years, both in the United States and elsewhere, with the recession of public support programs and the rise of punitive notions of the public good. Now families are expected to support their members, to raise their children to responsible adulthood, under the threat of local, state, and federal laws and private suits if they "fail." The making of citizens has become privatized as never before, subcontracted to families without means to make a go of it.

The most significant challenge to privatized/naturalized family has been the response of gay communities to AIDS. Gays and lesbians around the world have created organizations that extend the caring functions of family to those in need, which has in turn produced real changes in participants' ideas about who is family. Unfortunately, however, like many feminist cooperatives, the very success of these organizations at acquiring state funding has led them to adopt dominant goals and imperatives. Governmental preferences for research and prevention programs (not to mention criminal law) over care for people living with HIV or AIDS has meant that the original "family"-focused organizations have given way to corporate campaigns that no longer challenge ideas of kinship.

This second element of queering citizenship is intimately related to the first: the end of the phallic citizen. A central element of phallic citizenship is the illusion that one is self-sufficient and the demand that others be as well. Although cultures are not like philosophies, with ideas neatly placed in alignment and checked for consistency, we can nonetheless see integral relations between dominant ideas about citizenship and kinship and those concerning race, gender, and sexuality. The persistent intertwinement of gender, race, and sexuality in modern America, and the extensively documented relations between each of these and citizenship and kinship, make clear that citizenship cannot be queered without confronting the structures of gender and race through which it is constructed. This is the persistent problem with strategies of entry that do not simultaneously account for gender and race: not only will they fail to achieve entry for those marked by those other structures, they will fail to make room for the ever-persistent blooms of strangeness within white middle-class gay men. Few are those who can be so confident that new blossoms will never grow in their soil. Queering citizenship, then, must be more than citizenship for queers—not because the latter is not good enough, but because it cannot be achieved without the former. While many lesbians and gays will achieve greater recognition and acceptance, the terms of that recognition will continually place them at risk of re-othering.

The hidden links among kinship, citizenship, and bodies reside in our conceptions of what passions are appropriate in which areas of our lives. Queering citizenship will require a refocusing of the passions of citizenship. Currently the passions of adhesion—love (whether homosocial, familial, sexual, or all of these), empathy, desire—are slotted into compartments that hide their force in the construction of a common world. They are not absent, as liberals might hope and their critics might charge, but they are manipulated and interlaced with fear, anger, arrogance, and other "masculine" passions. Rather than building a foundation for republican government, the adhesive passions are reserved for the "private" world unless they can be marshaled to inspire unthinking support for government policy. And it is precisely their inevitable visibility in lesbian and gay politics that makes that politics so viscerally unnerving for so many. While all social movements must build on adhesive passions to form circles of solidarity, most movements continue to deny the bodily and sexual components of those passions. The love of co-protesters, we might say, is purely Platonic. But the rallying cry of lesbian and gay demonstrations—"an army of lovers cannot fail"—belies this sublimation/denial. Not only are gays and lesbians marked by their eroticism; queers who avow this eroticism in public (and not just the sanitized or regulated kinship forms through which the flow of eroticism is authorized) begin to demonstrate the presence of this eroticism in all collective endeavors. This does not mean that queers "don't do" anger, fear, or other "masculine" passions, but rather that they combine them in ways that do not disavow their links to adhesive passions. Queer citizenship must make room not only for a spectrum of bodies and comportments, but also for new arrangements of passions. The masculine republican citizen must give way to a citizen neither infantile nor stereotypically feminine, but capable of acknowledging and thriving on the adhesive passions, using them to overcome fears and angers that have been the signature passions of our times. The democratizing force of "emotions" described by Nicholson must be combined with an "ethos of pluralization" to foster not only attention and respect for emotions in others, but a new receptiveness to the play of unruly passions in ourselves. Rather than becoming "virtually normal," Americans must seek out the strange and the unexpected in themselves and others.

Most readers will likely recognize the magnitude of such a project, and surely the immediate chances for making such changes do not seem good. But cultural change is always a matter of gradual introductions of changes that do not seem possible until they happen. Although there is ample room for pessimism concerning the future of the United States and its citizens, that room will only increase if we do not imagine another future. It may well be that those who are currently sexual strangers will continue to be so for the duration of the American republic, and well past it. I mean to suggest here not "what should be done" in order to guarantee the end (which means the universalization) of strangerhood, but to fire imaginations stunted by an overdose of American politics. As Connolly (1995, xiii) phrases it, I choose to "give priority to possibility over probability because closures in the pluralist imagination itself help to conceal or marginalize injuries and limits in need of political engagement." As the old feminist motto says, women who aspire to be equal to men don't aim high enough. Sexual strangers who want to be the citizens currently on model sell themselves, and everyone else, short. Let's wait for a better offer.

Notes

Notes to Chapter 2

1. I do not mean to ignore examples of more personal love, such as that imagined by Plato through the character of Phaedrus: "If only there were a way to start a city of an army made up of lovers and the boys they love! Theirs would be the best possible system of society, for they would hold back from all that is shameful, and seek honor in each other's eyes" (*Symposium*, 179a). However, these examples rarely make their way from the philosophical literature to public discourse.

2. This endangered male is publicly presented as white, but white men are not the only ones suffering and reacting to the challenge. Black men, whose unemployment rates dwarf those of white men, have responded to calls for patriarchal masculinity such as the Million Man March. Chicano/Latino men are perhaps too diverse a group to characterize, but the ideal of the patriarchal provider continues to be central to many communities. I am not sufficiently educated on other groups to make generalizations about them, but I suspect that any group beyond first-generation immigrants encounters the hegemonic American masculine self and somehow is forced to negotiate with it.

Notes to Chapter 4

1. I do not include here more specialized books such as William Eskridge's *The Case for Same-Sex Marriage* (1996), which presumes a support for equality that is argued in the other books. My focus here is on the general issue of inclusion. The marriage issue deserves an analysis of its own; see Eskridge 1996 and Warner 1999.

2. The outstanding exception to this pattern is Urvashi Vaid (1995), who is critical of liberal individualism (though she does not abandon notions of rights and liberty) as well as prevailing gender and racial hierarchies. Torie Osborn (1996) also makes some critical mention of gender inequality, but her insistently upbeat message prevents her from being too critical.

3. In a different context, Annamarie Jagose (1994) refers to "straightened" presentations of lesbianism as the "transparent closet." In this closet, one is visibly lesbian, yet the terms of one's self-description are resolutely heterosexual. Although

163

this is not the place for an extended discussion, I refer the reader to Jagose's discussion in chapter 4.

Notes to Chapter 6

1. I am indebted to David Rayside for his complication of the idea and value of assimilation.

2. This is not to suggest that such critics as Christopher Lasch, Russell Jacoby, and others have no real point. Indeed, as Nicholson notes, many of them have importantly contributed to the critique of individualism in American life. By aligning individualism so exclusively with the emotions and new social movements, however, such critics reveal an uninterrogated kinship with conservatives.

Bibliography

Alexander, Jacqui. 1991. "Redrafting Sexual Morality: Trinidad and Tobago." In *Third World Women and the Politics of Feminism*, ed. Chandra T. Mohanty, Lourdes Torres, and Ann Russo. Bloomington: Indiana University Press.

———. 1994. "Not Just (Any) Body Can Be a Citizen: The Politics of Law, Sexuality and Postcoloniality in Trinidad and Tobago and the Bahamas." *Feminist Review* 48:5–23.

Altman, Dennis. 1981. *Coming Out in the Seventies*. Boston: Alyson.

Alwood, Edward. 1996. *Straight News: Lesbians, Gays, and the News Media*. New York: Columbia University Press.

Amnesty International USA. 1994. *Breaking the Silence: Human Rights Violations Based on Sexual Orientation*. New York: Amnesty International Publications.

Arendt, Hannah. 1966. *The Origins of Totalitarianism*. New York: Harcourt and Brace.

———. 1978. *The Jew as Pariah*. Ed. Ron Feldman. New York: Grove.

Aristotle. 1911. *The Politics*. Trans. Horace Rackham. Cambridge, MA: Harvard University Press.

Barber, Benjamin. 1984. *Strong Democracy*. Berkeley: University of California Press.

Barnard, Ian. 1996. "Queerzines and the Fragmentation of Art, Community, Identity, and Politics." *Socialist Review* 26/1–2:69–95.

Bauman, Zygmunt. 1988. *Postmodern Ethics*. Oxford: Basil Blackwell.

———. 1991. *Modernity and Ambivalence*. Ithaca, NY: Cornell University Press.

Bawer, Bruce. 1993. *A Place at the Table: The Gay Individual in American Society*. New York: Simon and Schuster.

Beck, Ulrich. 1996. "How Neighbors Become Jews: The Political Construction of the Stranger in an Age of Reflexive Modernity." *Constellations* 2/3:378–96.

Beiner, Ronald, ed. 1995. *Theorizing Citizenship*. Albany: State University of New York Press.

Benecke, Michelle M., and Kirstin S. Dodge. 1996. "Military Women: Casualties of the Armed Forces' War on Lesbians and Gay Men." In *Gay Rights, Military Wrongs: Political Perspectives on Lesbians and Gays in the Military*, ed. Craig Rimmerman. New York: Garland.

Benhabib, Seyla. 1992. "Models of Public Space: Hannah Arendt, the Liberal Tradition, and Jürgen Habermas." In *Habermas and the Public Sphere*, ed. Craig Calhoun. Cambridge, MA: MIT Press.

———. 1995. *The Reluctant Modernism of Hannah Arendt*. Newbury Park, CA: Sage.

Bennett, Lisa. 1998. "The Perpetuation of Prejudice in Reporting on Gays and Lesbians (*Time* and *Newsweek*: The First Fifty Years)." Research Paper R-21, Joan Shorenstein Center on the Press, Politics, and Public Policy, John F. Kennedy School of Government, Harvard University.

Berlant, Lauren. 1997. *The Queen of America Goes to Washington City: Essays on Sex and Citizenship*. Durham, NC: Duke University Press.

Bersani, Leo. 1995. *Homos*. Cambridge, MA: Harvard University Press.

Bianco, David Ari. 1996. "Echoes of Prejudice: The Debates over Race and Sexuality in the Armed Forces." In *Gay Rights, Military Wrongs*, ed. Craig Rimmerman, 47–70. New York: Garland.

Blasius, Mark, and Shane Phelan, eds. 1997. *We Are Everywhere: A Historical Sourcebook of Gay and Lesbian Politics*. New York: Routledge.

Boling, Patricia. 1996. *Privacy and the Politics of Intimate Life*. Ithaca, NY: Cornell University Press.

Bond, Justin. 1991. "Queer: Interviews." *Out/Look* 11:14,16.

Bordo, Susan. 1993. *Unbearable Weight: Feminism, Western Culture, and the Body*. Berkeley: University of California Press.

———. 1997. "Reading the Male Body." In *Building Bodies*, ed. Pamela Moore. New Brunswick, NJ: Rutgers University Press.

Boswell, John.1980. *Christianity, Social Tolerance, and Homosexuality: Gay People in Western Europe from the Beginning of the Christian Era to the Fourteenth Century*. Chicago: University of Chicago Press.

———. 1994. *Same-Sex Unions in Premodern Europe*. New York: Vintage.

Brettschneider, Marla. 1996. *Cornerstones of Peace: Jewish Identity Politics and Democratic Theory*. New Brunswick, NJ: Rutgers University Press.

Bristow, Joseph, and Angelia R. Wilson, eds. *Activating Theory: Lesbian, Gay, Bisexual Politics*. London: Lawrence and Wishart.

Brown, Wendy. 1995. "Wounded Attachments: Late Modern Oppositional Political Formations." In *The Identity in Question*, ed. John Rajchman. New York: Routledge.

Brubaker, Rogers. 1998. "Immigration, Citizenship, and the Nation-State in France and Germany." In *The Citizenship Debates*, ed. Gershon Shafir, 131–64. Minneapolis: University of Minnesota Press.

Burana, Lily, Roxxie, and Linnea Due, eds. 1994. *Dagger: On Butch Women*. San Francisco: Cleis Press.

Butler, Judith. 1990. *Gender Trouble: Feminism and the Subversion of Identity*. New York: Routledge.

———. 1991. "Imitation and Gender Insubordination." In *Inside/Out: Lesbian Theories, Gay Theories*, ed. Diana Fuss. New York: Routledge.

———. 1993. *Bodies That Matter*. New York: Routledge.

Calhoun, Craig, ed. 1992. *The Phantom Public Sphere*. Cambridge, MA: MIT Press.

Califia, Pat. 1994. *Public Sex: The Culture of Radical Sex*. Pittsburgh: Cleis Press.

Cammermeyer, Margaret, with Chris Fisher. 1994. *Serving in Silence*. New York: Viking.

Card, Claudia. 1995. *Lesbian Choices*. New York: Columbia University Press.

Carver, Terrell. 1996. "'Public Man' and the Critique of Masculinities." *Political Theory* 24/4:673–86.

Chapman, Kathleen, and Michael Du Plessis. 1997. "'Don't Call Me *Girl*': Lesbian Theory, Feminist Theory, and Transsexual Identities." In *Cross Purposes: Lesbians, Feminists, and the Limits of Alliance*, ed. Dana Heller, 169–85. Bloomington: Indiana University Press.

Cicchino, Peter M., Bruce R. Deming, and Katherine M. Nicholson. 1995. "Sex, Lies, and Civil Rights: A Critical History of the Massachusetts Gay Civil Rights Bill." In *Legal Inversions: Lesbians, Gay Men, and the Politics of Law*, ed. Didi Herman and Carl Stychin, 141–61. Philadelphia: Temple University Press.

Cohen, Cathy. 1999. *The Boundaries of Blackness*. Chicago: University of Chicago Press.

Comstock, Gary David. 1991. *Violence against Lesbians and Gay Men*. New York: Columbia University Press.

Connell, R.W. 1987. *Gender and Power*. Sydney: Allen and Unwin.

———. 1995. *Masculinities*. Berkeley: University of California Press.

Connolly, William E. 1995. *The Ethos of Pluralization*. Minneapolis: University of Minnesota Press.

Cook, Timothy. 1999. "Empirical Research on Lesbians and Gays in Politics." *American Political Science Review* 93/2.

Cook, Timothy, and Bevin Hartnett. 1999. "Splitting Image: The Nightly Network News and the Politics of the Lesbian and Gay Movement, 1969–1981." Paper presented at the meetings of the International Communication Association, San Francisco, May.

Cooper, Davina. 1993. "An Engaged State: Sexuality, Governance and the Potential for Change." In *Activating Theory*, ed. Joseph Bristow and Angelia Wilson, 190–218. London: Lawrence and Wishart.

Crittenden, S. H. 1957. *Report of the Board Appointed to Prepare and Submit Recommendations to the Secretary of the Navy for the Revision of Policies, Procedures and Directives Dealing with Homosexuality*. Washington, DC: Government Printing Office.

Currah, Paisley. 1996. "Searching for Immutability: Homosexuality, Race and Rights Discourse." In *A Simple Matter of Justice?* ed. Angelia R. Wilson. London: Cassell.

Curthoys, Ann. 1993. "Feminism, Citizenship and National Identity." *Feminist Review* 44:19–38.

D'Amico, Francine. 1996. "Race-ing and Gendering the Military Closet." In *Gay Rights, Military Wrongs: Political Perspectives on Lesbians and Gays in the Military*, ed. Craig Rimmerman. New York: Garland.

Davis, Angela. 1983. *Women, Race, and Class*. New York: Vintage.

Daumer, Elizabeth. 1992. "Queer Ethics, or The Challenge of Bisexuality to Lesbian Ethics." *Hypatia: A Journal of Feminist Philosophy* 7/4:91–105.

Dean, Jodi. 1996. *Solidarity of Strangers: Feminism after Identity Politics*. Berkeley: University of California Press.

de Lauretis, Teresa. 1991. "Queer Theory: Lesbian and Gay Sexualities: An Introduction," *differences: Journal of Feminist Cultural Studies* 3/2:iii–xviii.

D'Emilio, John. 1983. *Sexual Politics, Sexual Communities.* Chicago: University of Chicago Press.

D'Emilio, John, and Estelle Freedman. 1988. *Intimate Matters: A History of Sexuality in America.* New York: Harper and Row.

Deutchman, Iva E. 1998. "It's (Not) Just the Victim in Me: Gender and Power in the 1990s." *Women and Politics* 19/1:1–18.

Diner, Dan. 1998. "Nation, Migration, and Memory." *Constellations* 4/3:293–306.

Disch, Lisa. 1994. *Hannah Arendt and the Limits of Philosophy.* Ithaca, NY: Cornell University Press.

Doty, Alexander. 1993. *Making Things Perfectly Queer: Interpreting Mass Culture.* Minneapolis: University of Minnesota Press.

Dryzek, John. 1996. "Political Inclusion and the Dynamics of Democratization." *American Political Science Review* 90/3:475–87.

Dubiel, Helmut. 1998. "The Future of Citizenship in Europe." *Constellations* 4/3:368–373.

Dufour, Claude. 1995. "Comparative Analysis of Gay and Lesbian Rights Movements in Canada, the United States, and Australia." Ph.D. diss. University of Illinois at Chicago.

Duggan, Lisa. 1994. "Queering the State." *Social Text* 39:1–14.

Dunlap, Sue, and Kathleen Jones. 1996. "Queer Citizenship/Queer Representation: Politics out of Bounds?" Paper presented at the 1996 meetings of the American Political Science Association, San Francisco, CA, August 29–September 1.

Eadie, Jo. 1993. "Activating Bisexuality: Towards a Bi/Sexual Politics." In *Activating Theory: Lesbian, Gay, Bisexual Politics,* ed. Joseph Bristow and Angelia Wilson. London: Lawrence and Wishart.

Easthope, Anthony. 1986. *What a Man's Gotta Do: Masculinity in Popular Culture.* London: Palatin.

Edelman, Murray. 1964. *The Symbolic Uses of Politics.* Urbana: University of Illinois Press.

Elshtain, Jean Bethke. 1982. *Public Man, Private Woman.* Princeton, NJ: Princeton University Press.

Elshtain, Jean Bethke, and Sheila Tobias, eds. 1990. *Women, Militarism, and War.* Savage, MD: Rowman and Littlefield.

Engels, Friedrich. 1972 [1884]. *The Origins of Family, Private Property, and the State.* New York: Pathfinder.

Enloe, Cynthia. 1990. *Bananas, Beaches, and Bases: Making Feminist Sense of International Politics.* Berkeley: University of California Press.

———. 1993. *The Morning After: Sexual Politics at the End of the Cold War.* Berkeley: University of California Press.

Epstein, Steven. 1999. "Gay and Lesbian Movements in the United States: Dilemmas of Identity, Diversity, and Political Strategy." In *The Global Emergence of Gay and Lesbian Politics,* ed. Barry Adam, Jan Willem Duyvendak, and Andre Krouwel. Philadelphia: Temple University Press.

Eskridge, William N., Jr. 1996. *The Case for Same-Sex Marriage: From Sexual Liberty to Civilized Commitment.* New York: Free Press.

Etzioni, Amitai, ed. 1995. *New Communitarian Thinking.* Charlottesville: University of Virginia Press.

Evans, David T. 1993. *Sexual Citizenship: The Material Construction of Sexualities*. London: Routledge.

Faderman, Lillian 1991. *Odd Girls and Twilight Lovers: A History of Lesbian Life in Twentieth Century America*. New York: Columbia University Press.

Fish, Stanley. 1999. *The Trouble with Principle*. Cambridge, MA: Harvard University Press.

Forment, Carlos. 1995. "Peripheral Peoples and Narrative Identities: Arendtian Reflections on Late Modernity." In *Democracy and Difference*, ed. Seyla Benhabib, 314–30. Princeton, NJ: Princeton University Press.

Foucault, Michel. 1978. *The History of Sexuality*, vol. 1, *An Introduction*. New York: Pantheon.

Fraser, Nancy. 1992. "Rethinking the Public Sphere." In *Habermas and the Public Sphere*, ed. Craig Calhoun. Cambridge MA: MIT Press.

Fraser, Nancy, and Linda Gordon. 1994a. "A Genealogy of Dependency: Tracing a Keyword of the U.S. Welfare State." *Signs: Journal of Women in Culture and Society* 19:1–29.

———. 1994b. "Civil Citizenship against Social Citizenship?" In *The Condition of Citizenship*, ed. Bart van Steenburgen. London: Sage.

———. 1998. "Contract versus Charity: Why Is There No Social Citizenship in the United States?" In *The Citizenship Debates*, ed. Gershon Shafir. Minneapolis: University of Minnesota Press.

Galston, William. 1991. *Liberal Purposes*. Cambridge: Cambridge University Press.

Gamson, Joshua. 1996. "Must Identity Movements Self-Destruct?" In *Queer Theory/Sociology*, ed. Steven Seidman. Cambridge, MA: Blackwell.

———. 1998. *Freaks Talk Back: Tabloid Talk Shows and Sexual Nonconformity*. Chicago: University of Chicago Press.

Gatens, Moira. 1991. "Corporeal Representation in/and the Body Politic." In *Cartographies: Poststructuralism and the Mapping of Bodies and Spaces*, ed. Rosalyn Diprose and Robyn Ferrell. Sydney: Allen and Unwin.

General Accounting Office. 1992. *Defense Force Management: Statistics Related to DOD's Policy on Homosexuality*. Washington, DC: USGAO.

———. 1993. *Homosexuals in the Military: Policies and Practices of Foreign Countries*. Washington, DC: General Accounting Office.

Gilman, Sander. 1985. *Difference and Pathology*. Ithaca, NY: Cornell University Press.

———. 1991. *The Jew's Body*. New York: Routledge.

Gingrich, Candace, with Chris Bull. 1996. *The Accidental Activist*. New York: Touchstone.

Goffman, Erving. 1963. *Stigma: Notes on the Management of Spoiled Identity*. Englewood Cliffs, NJ: Prentice-Hall.

Goldberg-Hiller, Jonathan. 1998. "The Status of Status." Paper presented at Conference on Gender, Sexuality and the Law, Keele University, June 1998.

Goss, Robert E., and Amy Adams Squire Strongheart, eds. 1997. *Our Families, Our Values: Snapshots of Queer Kinship*. Binghamton, NY: Harrington Park.

Grosz, Elizabeth. 1994. *Volatile Bodies: Toward a Corporeal Feminism*. Bloomington: Indiana University Press.

Habermas, Jürgen. 1989. *The Structural Transformation of the Public Sphere*. Cambridge, MA: MIT Press.

————. 1995. "Citizenship and National Identity: Some Reflections on the Future of Europe." In *Theorizing Citizenship*, ed. Ronald Beiner. Albany: State University of New York Press.

Haider-Markel, Donald P., and Kenneth J. Meier. 1996. " The Politics of Gay and Lesbian Rights: Expanding the Scope of the Conflict." *Journal of Politics* 58 (May): 332–49.

Halberstam, Judith. 1998. *Female Masculinity*. Durham, NC: Duke University Press.

Hale, C. Jacob. 1998. "Consuming the Living, Dis(re)membering the Dead in the Butch/Ftm Borderlands." *GLQ: A Journal of Lesbian and Gay Studies* 4/2:311–48.

Halperin, David. *One Hundred Years of Homosexuality, and Other Essays on Greek Love*. New York: Routledge, 1989.

Halvorsen, Rune. 1998. "The Ambiguity of Lesbian and Gay Marriages: Change and Continuity in the Symbolic Order." *Journal of Homosexuality* 35/3–4:207–31.

Hartsock, Nancy. 1983. *Money, Sex, and Power*. Boston: Northeastern University Press.

Hegel, G.W.F. 1979. *The Philosophy of Right*. Trans. T. M. Knox. Oxford: Oxford University Press.

Hennessy, Rosemary. 1995. "Queer Visibility and Commodity Culture." In *Social Postmodernisn*, ed. Linda Nicholson and Steven Seidman, 142–83. Cambridge: Cambridge University Press.

Herek, Gregory K., and Kevin Berrill. 1992. *Hate Crimes: Confronting Violence against Lesbians and Gay Men*. Newbury Park, CA: Sage.

Herman, Didi. 1997. *The Anti-Gay Agenda: Orthodox Vision and the Christian Right*. Chicago: University of Chicago Press.

Herman, Didi, and Carl Stychin. 1995. *Legal Inversions: Lesbians, Gay Men, and the Politics of Law*. Philadelphia: Temple University Press.

Hertzog, Mark. 1996. *The Lavender Vote: Lesbians, Gay Men, and Bisexuals in American Electoral Politics*. New York: New York University Press.

Highleyman, Liz A. 1995. "Identity and Ideas: Strategies for Bisexuals." In *Bisexual Politics: Theories, Queries, and Visions*, ed. Naomi Tucker with Liz Highleyman and Rebecca Kaplan, 73–92. New York: Harrington Park Press.

Hinchman, Lewis P., and Sandra K. Hinchman. 1994. *Hannah Arendt: Critical Essays*. Albany: State University of New York Press.

Honig, Bonnie. 1995. *Feminist Interpretations of Hannah Arendt*. University Park: Pennsylvania State University Press.

hooks, bell. 1981. *Ain't I a Woman: Black Women and Feminism*. Boston: South End.

Humphrey, Mary Ann. 1990. *My Country, My Right to Serve: Experiences of Gay Men and Women in the Military, World War II to the Present*. New York: HarperCollins.

Ignatieff, Michael. 1995. "The Myth of Citizenship." In *Theorizing Citizenship*, ed. Ronald Beiner, 53–78. Albany: State University of New York Press.

Inness, Sherrie, and Michele E. Lloyd. 1996. "G.I. Joes in Barbie Land: Recontextualizing Butch in Twentieth-Century Lesbian Culture." In *Queer Studies*, ed. Brett Beemyn and Mickey Eliason, 7–34. New York: New York University Press.

Irigaray, Luce. 1985. *Speculum of the Other Woman*. Trans. Gillian C. Gill. Ithaca, NY: Cornell University Press.

Jagose, Annamarie. 1994. *Lesbian Utopics*. New York: Routledge.

Jay, Karla, and Allen Young. 1972. *Out of the Closets: Voices of Gay Liberation*. New York: Douglas.

Jeffreys, Sheila. 1993. *The Lesbian Heresy*. North Melbourne: Spinifex.

————. 1997. "Transgender Activism: A Lesbian Feminist Perspective." *Journal of Lesbian Studies* 1/3–4:55–74.

Jones, Kathleen. 1997. "Citizenship in Feminism: Identity, Action, and Locale: An Introduction." *Hypatia: A Journal of Feminist Philosophy* 12/4:1–5.

————. 1998. "Citizenship in a Woman-Friendly Polity." In *The Citizenship Debates*, ed. Gershon Shafir, 221–50. Minneapolis: University of Minnesota Press.

Kaplan, Morris. 1997. *Sexual Justice: Democratic Citizenship and the Politics of Desire.* New York: Routledge.

Katzenstein, Mary Fainsod. 1996. "The Spectacle of Life and Death: Feminist and Lesbian/Gay Politics in the Military." In *Gay Rights, Military Wrongs: Political Perspectives on Lesbians and Gays in the Military*, ed. Craig Rimmerman. New York: Garland.

Kennedy, Elizabeth Lapovsky, and Madeline Davis. 1993. *Boots of Leather, Slippers of Gold: The History of a Lesbian Community.* New York: Routledge.

Kerber, Linda. 1997. *Toward an Intellectual History of Women.* Chapel Hill: University of North Carolina Press.

Kirk, Marshall, and Hunter Madsen. 1989. *After the Ball: How America Will Conquer Its Fear and Hatred of Gays in the 1990s.* New York: Penguin Books.

Kitzinger, Celia. 1987. *The Social Construction of Lesbianism.* London: Sage.

Kristeva, Julia. 1982. *Powers of Horror.* New York: Columbia University Press.

————. 1991. *Strangers to Ourselves.* Trans. Leon S. Roudiez. New York: Columbia University Press.

Laclau, Ernesto, and Chantal Mouffe. 1985. *Hegemony and Socialist Strategy.* London: Verso.

Leca, Jean. 1992. "Questions on Citizenship." In *Dimensions of Radical Democracy*, ed. Chantal Mouffe. London: Verso.

Lehning, Percy B. 1998. "European Citizenship: Between Facts and Norms." *Constellations* 4/3:346–67.

Lehr, Valerie. 1999. *Queer Family Values: Debunking the Myth of the Nuclear Family.* Philadelphia: Temple University Press.

Lehring, Gary. 1997. "Essentialism and the Political Articulation of Identity." In *Playing with Fire: Queer Politics, Queer Theories*, ed. Shane Phelan, 173–98. New York: Routledge.

Lewin, Ellen. 1993. *Lesbian Mothers: Accounts of Gender in American Culture.* Ithaca, NY: Cornell University Press.

————. 1998. *Recognizing Ourselves: Ceremonies of Lesbian and Gay Commitment.* New York: Columbia University Press.

Likosky, Stephan. 1992. *Out in the World.* New York: Vintage.

Lincoln, Abraham. 1992. *Selected Writings.* Ed. with an introduction by Herbert Mitgang. New York: Bantam.

Lister, Ruth. 1997. *Citizenship: Feminist Perspectives.* New York: New York University Press.

Lorde, Audre. 1984. *Sister Outsider.* Trumansburg, NY: Crossing Press.

Loulan, JoAnn. 1990. *The Lesbian Erotic Dance: Butch, Femme, Androgyny, and Other Rhythms.* San Francisco: Spinsters.

Lugones, Maria, and Elizabeth Spelman. 1983. "Have We Got a Theory for You! Feminist Theory, Cultural Imperialism and the Demand for 'the Woman's Voice.'" *Women's Studies International Forum* 6: 573–81.

Luibheid, Eithne. 1995. "'Obvious Homosexuals and Homosexuals Who Cover Up': Lesbian and Gay Exclusion in US Immigration." *Gay Community News* 20(5):17–20.

Lumsden, Ian. 1996. *Machos, Maricones, and Gays: Cuba and Homosexuality.* Philadelphia: Temple University Press.

Lyotard, Jean-François, and Jean-Loup Thebaud. 1985. *Just Gaming.* Minneapolis: University of Minnesota Press.

Marshall, T.M. 1992. "Citizenship and Social Class." In T.M. Marshall and Tom Bottomore, *Citizenship and Social Class.* London: Pluto.

Martin, Biddy. 1994. "Sexualities without Genders and Other Queer Utopias." *diacritics* 24/2–3:104–21.

Minow, Martha. 1990. *Making All the Difference: Inclusion, Exclusion, and American Law.* Ithaca, NY: Cornell University Press.

Mohr, Richard. 1988. *Gays/Justice.* New York: Columbia University Press.

———. 1994. *A More Perfect Union: Why Straight America Must Stand Up for Gay Rights.* Boston: Beacon.

———. 1997. "The Case for Gay Marriage." In Robert M. Baird and Stuart E. Rosenbaum eds., *Same-Sex Marriage: The Moral and Legal Debate.* Amherst, MA: Prometheus Books.

———. 1999. "A Gay and Straight Agenda." In *Same Sex: Debating the Ethics, Science, and Culture of Homosexuality,* ed. John Corvino. Lanham, MD: Rowman and Littlefield.

Monoson, Sara. 1994. "Citizen as Erastes: Erotic Imagery and the Idea of Reciprocity in the Periclean Funeral Oration." *Political Theory* 22/2:253–76.

Morgan, Tracy. 1993. "Butch-Femme and the Politics of Identity." In *Sisters, Sexperts, Queers: Beyond the Lesbian Nation.* ed. Arlene Stein. New York: Plume.

Morrison, Toni. 1992. *Race-ing Justice, En-Gendering Power.* New York: Pantheon.

Mosse, George. 1985. *Nationalism and Sexuality.* New York: Howard Fertig.

Mouffe, Chantal, ed. 1992. *Dimensions of Radical Democracy.* London: Verso.

———. 1993. *The Return of the Political.* London: Verso.

Namaste, Ki. 1997. "'Tragic Misreadings': Queer Theory's Erasure of Transgender Subjectivity." In *Queer Studies: A Lesbian, Gay, Bisexual, and Transgender Anthology,* ed. Brett Beemyn and Mickey Eliason. New York: New York University Press.

Nataf, Zachary I. 1996. *Lesbians Talk Transgender.* London: Scarlet.

Nava, Michael, and Robert Dawidoff. *Created Equal: Why Gay Rights Matter to America.* New York: St. Martin's Press.

Nestle, Joan. 1992. "The Fem Question," in *The Persistent Desire: A Femme-Butch Reader,* ed. Joan Nestle. Boston: Alyson.

Newton, Esther. 1984. "The Mythic Mannish Lesbian: Radclyffe Hall and the New Woman." *Signs: Journal of Women in Culture and Society* 9/4:557–75.

Nicholson, Linda. 1999. *The Play of Reason: From the Modern to the Postmodern.* Ithaca, NY: Cornell University Press.

O'Donnell, Shauna Maile. 1996. "A New Choreography of Sexual Difference, or Just the Same Old Song and Dance?" *Socialist Review* 25(1):95–118.

Okin, Susan. 1989. *Justice, Gender, and the Family.* New York: Basic Books.

Oldfield, Gary. 1998. "Citizenship and Community: Civic Republicanism and the Modern World." In *The Citizenship Debates,* ed. Gershon Shafir, 75–92. Minneapolis: University of Minnesota Press.

Omi, Michael, and Howard Winant. 1986. *Racial Formation in the United States from the 1960s to the 1980s*. New York: Routledge.

O'Neill, John. 1985. *Five Bodies*. Ithaca, NY: Cornell University Press.

Osborn, Torie. 1996. *Coming Home to America*. New York: St. Martin's Press.

Pacelle, Richard. 1996. "Seeking Another Forum: The Courts and Lesbian and Gay Rights." In *Gay Rights, Military Wrongs: Political Perspectives on Lesbians and Gays in the Military*, ed. Craig Rimmerman. New York: Garland.

Parker, Andrew, Mary Russo, Doris Sommer, and Patricia Yaeger. 1992. *Nationalisms and Sexualities*. New York: Routledge.

Pateman, Carole. 1988. *The Sexual Contract*. Stanford, CA: Stanford University Press.

———. 1989. *The Disorder of Women*. Stanford, CA: Stanford University Press.

Peterson, V. Spike. 1999. "Sexing Political Identities/Nationalism as Heterosexism." *International Feminist Journal of Politics* 1/1:34–65.

Peterson, V. Spike, and Laura Parisi. 1997. "Are Women Human: It's Not an Academic Question." Paper presented at the Thirty-eighth Annual Meeting of the International Studies Association, Toronto.

Phelan, Shane. 1989. *Identity Politics: Lesbian Feminism and the Limits of Community*. Philadelphia: Temple University Press.

———. 1994. *Getting Specific: Postmodern Lesbian Politics*. Minneapolis: University of Minnesota Press.

———. 1996. "Coyote Politics: Trickster Tales and Feminist Futures." *Hypatia: A Journal of Feminist Philosophy* 11/3:130–149.

Phillips, Anne. 1991. *Engendering Democracy*. University Park: Pennsylvania State University Press.

Pitkin, Hannah Fenichel. 1984. *Fortune Is a Woman: Gender and Politics in the Thought of Niccolo Machiavelli*. Berkeley: University of California Press.

Plato. 1961. *The Symposium*, trans. Michael Joyce. In *The Collected Dialogues of Plato*, ed. Edith Hamilton and Huntington Cairns. Princeton, NJ: Princeton University Press.

Pocock, J.G.A. 1975. *The Machiavellian Moment: Florentine Political Thought and the Atlantic Republican Tradition*. Princeton, NJ: Princeton University Press.

———. 1998. "The Ideal of Citizenship Since Classical Times." In *The Citizenship Debates*, ed. Gershon Shafir. Minneapolis: University of Minnesota Press.

Pratt, Minnie Bruce. 1995. *S/he*. Ithaca, NY: Firebrand.

Preuss, Ulrich K. 1998. "Migration—A Challenge to Modern Citizenship." *Constellations* 4/3:307–19.

Prosser, Jay. 1998. *Second Skins: The Body Narratives of Transsexuality*. New York: Columbia University Press.

Quinby, Lee. 1999. "Virile-Reality: From Armageddon to Viagra." *Signs: Journal of Women in Culture and Society* 24/4:1079–87.

RAND. 1993. *Sexual Orientation and U.S. Military Personnel Policy: Options and Assessment*. Santa Monica, CA: RAND National Defense Research Institute.

Raymond, Janice. 1979. *The Transsexual Empire: The Making of the She-Male*. Boston: Beacon.

Rayside, David. 1998. *On the Fringe: Gays and Lesbians in Politics*. Ithaca, NY: Cornell University Press.

Rich, Adrienne. 1980. "Compulsory Heterosexuality and Lesbian Existence. *Signs: Journal of Women in Culture and Society* 5/1:631–660

Riesenberg, Peter. 1992. *Citizenship in the Western Tradition: Plato to Rousseau.* Chapel Hill: University of North Carolina Press.

Rimmerman, Craig, ed. 1996. *Gay Rights, Military Wrongs: Political Perspectives on Lesbians and Gays in the Military.* New York: Garland.

————. 1999b. "New Kids on the Block." In *Risky Business? PAC Decisionmaking in Congressional Elections.* ed. Robert Biersack, Paul Herrnson, and Clyde Wilcox. Armonk, NY: M. E. Sharpe.

Roosevelt, Theodore. 1958. *The Free Citizen: A Summons to Service of the Democratic Ideal.* Ed. Herman Hagedorn. New York: The Theodore Roosevelt Association.

Rousseau, Jean-Jacques. 1911. *Emile.* Trans. Barbara Foxley. New York: E. P. Dutton.

Rubin, Barry. 1995. *Assimilation and Its Discontents.* New York: Times Books.

Rubin, Gayle. 1984. "Thinking Sex: Notes for a Radical Theory of the Politics of Sexuality." In *Pleasure and Danger: Exploring Female Sexuality*, ed. Carole Vance. Boston: Routledge and Kegan Paul.

Rubin, Gayle, with Judith Butler. 1994. "Sexual Traffic." *differences: Journal of Feminist Cultural Studies* 6(2–3): 62–99.

Rust, Paula. 1995. *Bisexuality and the Challenge to Lesbian Politics: Sex, Loyalty, and Revolution.* New York: New York University Press.

Sandel, Michael. 1982. *Liberalism and the Limits of Justice.* Cambridge: Cambridge University Press.

————, ed. 1984. *Liberalism and Its Critics.* New York: New York University Press.

Sarvasy, Wendy. 1997. "Social Citizenship from a Feminist Perspective." *Hypatia: A Journal of Feminist Philosophy* 12/4:54–73.

Schatzki, Theodore R., and Wolfgang Natter, eds. 1996. *The Social and Political Body.* New York: Guilford.

Schilling, Chris. 1993. *The Body and Social Theory.* London: Sage.

Schneider, David. 1968. *American Kinship: A Cultural Account.* Englewood Cliffs, NJ: Prentice-Hall.

Schwartz, Joel. 1984. *The Sexual Politics of Jean-Jacques Rousseau.* Chicago: University of Chicago Press.

Scott, James. 1990. *Domination and the Arts of Resistance: Hidden Transcripts.* New Haven, CT: Yale University Press.

Sedgwick, Eve. 1990. *Epistemology of the Closet.* Berkeley: University of California Press.

————. 1993. *Tendencies.* Durham, NC: Duke University Press.

Shilts, Randy. 1993. *Conduct Unbecoming: Gays and Lesbians in the U.S. Military.* New York: St. Martin's Press.

Shklar, Judith. 1991. *American Citizenship: The Quest for Inclusion.* Cambridge, MA: Harvard University Press.

Shugar, Dana. 1995. *Separatism and Women's Community.* Lincoln: University of Nebraska Press.

Signorile, Michelangelo. 1997. *Life Outside—The Signorile Report on Gay Men: Sex, Drugs, Muscles, and the Passages of Life.* New York: HarperCollins.

Smith, Anna Marie. 1994a. "The Imaginary Inclusion of the Assimilable Immigrant and the 'Good Homosexual': The British New Right's Representation of Sexuality and Race." *Diacritics* 24(2–3):58–70.

————. 1994b. *New Right Discourse on Race and Sexuality: Britain, 1968–1990.* Cambridge: Cambridge University Press.

Smith, Rogers M. 1989. "One United People: Female Citizenship and the American Quest for Community." *Yale Journal of Law and the Humanities* 1:229–93.
———. 1997. *Civic Ideals: Conflicting Visions of Citizenship in U.S. History.* New Haven, CT: Yale University Press.
Sparks, Holloway. 1997. "Dissident Citizenship: Democratic Theory, Political Courage, and Activist Women." *Hypatia: A Journal of Feminist Philosophy* 12/4: 74–110.
Spinner, Brent. 1994. *The Boundaries of Citizenship: Race, Ethnicity, and Nationality in the Liberal State.* Baltimore: Johns Hopkins University Press.
Stacey, Judith. 1998. "Gay and Lesbian Families: Queer Like Us." In *All Our Families: New Policies for a New Century,* ed. Mary Ann Mason, Arlene Skolnick, and Stephen D. Sugarman. Oxford: Oxford University Press.
Steffan, Joseph. 1992. *Honor Bound: A Gay American Fights for the Right to Serve His Country.* New York: Villard.
Stein, Arlene, ed. 1993. *Sisters, Sexperts, Queers: Beyond the Lesbian Nation.* New York: Plume.
Stevens, Jacqueline. 1997. "On the Marriage Question." In *Women Transforming Politics: An Alternative Reader,* ed. Cathy J. Cohen, Kathleen B. Jones, and Joan C. Tronto. New York: New York University Press.
Stiehm, Judith. 1989. *Arms and the Enlisted Woman.* Philadelphia: Temple University Press.
Stryker, Susan. 1998. "The Transgender Issue: An Introduction." *GLQ: A Journal of Lesbian and Gay Studies* 4/2:145–58.
Stychin, Carl. 1998. *A Nation by Rights: National Cultures, Sexual Identity Politics, and the Discourse of Rights.* Philadelphia: Temple University Press.
Sullivan, Andrew. 1995. *Virtually Normal: An Argument about Homosexuality.* New York: Knopf.
Tafel, Richard. 1999. *Party Crasher: A Gay Republican Challenges Politics as Usual.* New York: Simon and Schuster.
Tassin, Etienne. 1992. "Europe: A Political Community?" In *Dimensions of Radical Democracy,* ed. Chantal Mouffe, 169–92. London: Verso.
Tatchell, Peter. 1995. *We Don't Want to March Straight: Masculinity, Queers and the Military.* London: Cassell.
Taylor, Charles. 1985. *Philosophical Essays,* 2 vols. Cambridge: Cambridge University Press.
———. 1994. *Multiculturalism: Examining the Politics of Recognition.* Princeton, NJ: Princeton University Press.
Tobin, Kay. 1965. "Picketing: The Impact and the Issues." *The Ladder* 9/12:4.
Trinh Minh-ha. 1990. *Woman, Native, Other.* Bloomington: Indiana University Press.
Tronto, Joan. 1993. *Moral Boundaries: A Political Argument for an Ethic of Care.* New York: Routledge.
Trujillo, Carla. 1991. *Chicana Lesbians: The Girls Our Mothers Warned Us About.* Berkeley: Third Woman Press.
Tucker, Naomi, ed. 1995. *Bisexual Politics: Theories, Queries, and Visions.* New York: Harrington Park.
Turner, Bryan. 1992. *Regulating Bodies.* London: Routledge.
———. 1994. "Postmodern Culture/Modern Citizens." In *The Condition of Citizenship,* ed. Bart van Steenbergen, 153–68. London: Sage.

U.S. Congress. House of Representatives. 1890. *Amendment to Section 5352, Revised Statutes.* 51st Cong., 1st sess, Report 1811.

——— 1902. *Polygamy.* Committee on the Judiciary. 57th Cong., 1st sess.

Vaid, Urvashi. 1995. *Virtual Equality: The Mainstreaming of Gay and Lesbian Liberation.* New York: Anchor.

Vicinus, Martha. 1992. "'They Wonder to Which Sex I Belong': The Historical Roots of the Modern Lesbian Identity." *Feminist Studies* 18/3: 467–97.

Vogel, Ursula. 1991. "Is Citizenship Gender-Specific?" In *The Frontiers of Citizenship*, ed. Ursula Vogel and Michael Moran. New York: St. Martin's Press.

———. 1994. "Marriage and the Boundaries of Citizenship." In *The Condition of Citizenship*, ed. Bart van Steenbergen, 76–89. London: Sage.

Waldby, Catherine. 1996. *AIDS and the Body Politic: Biomedicine and Sexual Difference.* London: Routledge.

Warner, Michael. 1993a. "The Mass Public and the Mass Subject." In *The Phantom Public Sphere*, ed. Bruce Robbins. Minneapolis: University of Minnesota Press.

———. 1993b. *Fear of a Queer Planet: Queer Politics and Social Theory.* Minneapolis: University of Minnesota Press.

———. 1999. "Normal and Normaller: Beyond Gay Marriage." *GLQ: A Journal of Lesbian and Gay Studies* 5/2:119–71.

Watney, Simon. 1996. *Policing Desire: Pornography, AIDS, and the Media.* 3d ed. Minneapolis: University of Minnesota Press.

Weber, Cynthia. 1999. *Faking It: U.S. Hegemony in a "Post-Phallic" Era.* Minneapolis: University of Minnesota Press.

Weston, Kath. 1991. *Families We Choose: Lesbians, Gays, and Kinship.* New York: Columbia University Press.

Wilcox, Clyde, and Robin M. Wolpert. 1996. "President Clinton, Public Opinion, and Gays in the Military." In *Gay Rights, Military Wrongs: Political Perspectives on Lesbians and Gays in the Military*, ed. Craig Rimmerman. New York and London: Garland.

Williams, Patricia. 1991. *The Alchemy of Race and Rights.* Cambridge, MA: Harvard University Press.

Wilson, Angelia. 1995. *A Simple Matter of Justice?* London: Cassell.

Wolinsky, Marc, and Kenneth Sherrill. 1993. *Gays and the Military: Joseph Steffan versus the United States.* Princeton, NJ: Princeton University Press.

Young, Allen. 1981. *Gays under the Cuban Revolution.* San Francisco: Grey Fox Press.

Young, Iris Marion. 1990. *Justice and the Politics of Difference.* Princeton, NJ: Princeton University Press.

———. 1995. "Communication and the Other: Beyond Deliberative Democracy." In *Democracy and Difference*, ed. Seyla Benhabib, 120–35. Princeton, NJ: Princeton University Press.

———. 1996. "Reflections on Families in the Age of Murphy Brown: On Gender, Justice, and Sexuality." In *Revisioning the Political*, ed. Nancy J. Hirschmann and Christine Di Stefano, 251–70. Boulder, CO: Westview.

———. 1997. *Intersecting Voices: Dilemmas of Gender, Political Philosophy, and Public Policy.* Princeton, NJ: Princeton University Press.

Young, Stacey. 1997. "Dichotomies and Displacement: Bisexuality in Queer Theory and Politics." In *Playing with Fire: Queer Politics, Queer Theories*, ed. Shane Phelan. New York: Routledge.

Index